M000280876

THE BOOK OF
BLESSINGS AND RITUALS

MAGICAL INVOCATIONS
FOR HEALING, SETTING ENERGY, AND
CREATING SACRED SPACE

Athena Perrakis, Ph.D.

FAIR WINDS

More praise for
The Book of Blessings and Rituals:

"From ancestral rituals to home healing altars,
The Book of Blessings and Rituals reads like sage
advice and insight from a gentle, magical friend. As the
moon changes shape, and as the seasons come and go,
the words in these pages will be there to guide you
toward your own magic and inner light."

—Lisa Marie Basile, author of *Light Magic for Dark Times*

"Beautiful blessings. Beautiful illustrations.
Beautiful book."

—Yasmin Boland, author of *Moonology*

Dedication

I dedicate this book to my Spirit Guides and the Plant Teachers, as these blessings and invocations were channeled from another realm, anchored in a wisdom that far exceeds my own. To my husband Dave, my children Nick and Zoe, and my Sage Goddess community who bring so much love and beauty to my life. The words here have led and nurtured us through many beautiful turnings of the Great Wheel of Time. I also dedicate this book to my team at Sage Goddess for their assistance in bringing the imagery here to life.

Finally, I dedicate this book to my grandchildren and all generations forward. These words belong to you, and I hope they will guide you in your practice. Always remember that magic is real; you simply need to trust, believe, and surrender. In body and one day in spirit, I am honored to be your ancestor and am doing my best to leave this planet in the best possible condition for you and yours. How I look forward to seeing where you take my magic as you embrace your own unique destinies. A'ho and on we go.

Contents

Introduction

This book is a collection of blessings, rituals, and invocations I have crafted since I gave birth to Sage Goddess in 2011. I have woven them into a sacred tapestry in hopes that the union of them will bless, inspire, and guide you.

I did not set out to write a book of blessings and rituals, which in many ways is what makes it so profound. These are not esoteric teachings sans applicability or relevance; these are uttered blessings and projects that have guided me and my students toward transformation and healing. Now, they belong to you.

This book is a doorway to your own magic. Enter with caution, gratitude, and excitement. May the threshold you are about to cross be a blessed one, my friend, and may you always remember the power of words. Choose them well and say them with strength. In that way, you will find your wisest voice and your deepest authentic truth, and on that same path you will bring honor and healing to your line.

Please note that this book is written in alignment with the cycles of the northern hemisphere. But brothers and sisters of the southern hemisphere, simply follow it in alignment with your cycles and you will find resonance and power within to support you.

Energy work is real, and all energy is composed of both light and shadow aspects. Although certain basic ceremonial protocols are woven into each project and ritual included here, you should always take the following precautions before *any* sacred practice:

- **Smudge** with cleansing herbs such as white sage, sacred trees such as palo santo, or resins such as copal and myrrh.
- **Open a sacred circle** by taking a selenite or other wand and opening a circle in the air, clockwise, asking that only energies in service to the Highest Good be allowed to enter therein.

- **Invite and thank the Guardians** of the Four Directions to attend your workings. Anchoring the four directions helps you create a tight container for your work, in which the energy you raise will be stronger and more likely to yield a good outcome.

Then, *after* any sacred practice:

- **Release the Guardians** of the Four Directions with gratitude, thanking them for their presence and wisdom.
- **Release your sacred circle** by turning your wand counterclockwise in a circle (either in the air or on the ground in front of you), giving thanks to the energies present for your work and releasing them with gratitude.
- **Smudge and ground** your own energy. Almandine garnet, when held in each hand, is an excellent anchoring crystal after a ceremony.

How long you work with an altar is up to you. If you feel called to keep it as a reminder and space for meditation, honor that instinct. Clean your altar at the new moon, recharging it with intention if you desire. Take altars down, also at the new moon, by removing items in the opposite order in which they were originally placed. The power of an altar waxes and wanes with the moon, and is thus strongest at the full moon; do not move or clear your altars within forty-eight hours of a full moon or during an eclipse, if possible. Keep your altar free of dust; sacred space is worthy of your attention.

Take care to honor important protocol in your practice. Not only will you be safer doing so, but also your magical work will be more efficacious. Consider the guidance here a series of general directions, however, and if your practice guides you differently, trust what feels right and accurate.

In preparation for our work together, a prayer:

Great Spirit, Wakan Tanka, Father God, Mother Goddess, Source, Creator, please activate the words on these pages so they embody the medicine and magic needed in the moment and reveal what must be known to the one who reads them. Let it be understood that it is the spirit of the reader, his or her unique essence, that brings my words to life. May the one who reads these words be blessed in all ways, always.

Amen, A'ho, and On we go

Athena

1

January

THE MONTH OF NEW BEGINNINGS

The pressure has been building since Samhain, since the fall equinox even. You have wanted to envision, imagine, and create since harvest season, but you have also honored the call to rest, the invitation to slumber that is the winter season in the northern hemisphere. Now you are in the thick of your dormancy, yet the fire within you still burns. This is the time to indulge your creative senses and set a powerful course for the year ahead. You get few clear shots at your dreams each year. This is one of them. Aim well, spirit traveler. But let your arrow go, eventually. If you spend your whole life aiming, you might as well not even engage the bow.

Trust in yourself is what makes January a dual blessing and challenge. When you released the fruits from your vines last September, you were rich with inspiration and gratitude. But now as you gaze across the vista of life, it is a darker and more barren place you see. In winter, hope must come from within. Relying on others, expecting outside reward or motivation, is risky now. Everything you will build in the year ahead already resides within you today. Now is the time to create, but in a passive way—for example, visualizing and setting intentions. Intentions are best set at the new year and the new moon, so you have multiple opportunities this month.

Take a moment now to be with the beginning of this new calendar year, present to both its possibilities and its challenges. Imagine yourself celebrating twelve months from now the desires, successes, and experiences you most seek. What do you need to allow, surrender, or invite right now to achieve your goals for the rest of the year? Ask your spirit guides, higher self, and all light beings to surround you, support you, and sustain you. May you receive all that you long for, in perfect time and full alignment with your intended path.

Y a'ho

— PRAYER —
Smudging

**To clear and cleanse your
sacred spaces, including
temples, sanctuaries,
homes, and classrooms**

*Guardians of the Plant and Tree Kingdoms,
sacred medicines of the jungle floor,
the outback, the desert, and the
river's edge.
We call upon all of our plant teachers
to share your wisdom, blessings, and
healing now.*

*As we burn your herbs, resins, leaves,
and limbs,
we invite you to come into our space
and release energies that are stuck or slow,
freeing us to move and grow
in alignment with our path, purpose,
and vision.
We thank you, plant teachers
Maestros de la Selva Oscura
for your wisdom and love.*

Amen, A'ho, So it is

— Invocation —
Four Directional

The original Sage Goddess invocation to the Guardians of the Four Directions

Between day and night, we gather and seek
the wisdom of the elders, the ancients, the guides,
the ancestors, and humbly in their presence, we seek the knowledge we are ready to integrate.
For this is the hour of magic,
and now is the moment of possibility.
Gatekeepers of the Four Directions, thank you for turning your gaze toward us this evening.
We honor your sacred presence
and thank you for your guidance.
For you are welcome here.
I call first to the guardians and gatekeepers of the East,
and to you, Libra, Aquarius, Gemini.
I call to Air,
to the white clouds wandering across a pale blue-violet sky
and to the air that lifts them.
To the breeze that blows across my face,
to warm summer currents that bring scents of sea and sand.
To the whispers of dawn,

ancient voices speaking in familiar tongues.
To the chilly blast of winter's breath,
to the hurricanes that destroy so we can re-create,
and to the currents that support the wings of the seagull.
To the winds of my dreams, carrying my hopes for tomorrow,
and to the storms of my heart, violent and tempestuous.
To desert gusts, where lightning strikes and thunder rumbles.
Be here with us tonight, element of air, and let the power of your gentle force fill our lungs, open our minds,
and lift our spirits.
I call to the guardians and gatekeepers of the South,
and to you, Aries, Leo, Sagittarius.
I call to Fire,
to the dry heat of the desert
that burns under a flaming orange sun.
To the courage of the lion whose red mane dances in golden majesty about his face,
and to the energy that burns within me and within you.
To the sparkles of fairy magic
and the golden glow of citrine stones.

To the flickering of the candle as it burns,
and to the lava flowing from wild and
    untamed volcanoes,
native and free.
To the bonfire around which we all gather
and vision quest together.
To the warmth of unconditional love we
    offer in this space, and to the sage we
    burn to clear, clean, and consecrate.
Be here with us tonight, element
    of fire, and let the power of your
    mighty force warm our hearts, release
    our fears,
and destroy our resistance to growth.
I call to the guardians and gatekeepers
    of the West,
and to you, Pisces, Cancer, Scorpio.
I call to Water,
to the deep blue-green waves that rush
    the shore.
To the dolphin who weaves in and out
    of the purple sea,
daring to explore the deepest waters,
and to the mermaid who is bound to
    the depths,
personifying flow and grace.
To the awesome power of currents that
    carry me forward, spiraling and
    gasping, into a future I dare to meet.
To the raging river running wild like
    my heart,
and to the azure lake where my children
    run at the water's edge.
To the rain in which we dance, together,
    fearless, letting go,

and to destiny as we gaze out over
    endless seas
that divide and connect us.
Be here with us tonight, element
    of water, and let the power of your
    graceful force wash us clean and
    teach us
to swim with the tide
rather than resist its pull.
Last, but never least,
I call to the guardians and gatekeepers
    of the North,
and to you, Virgo, Capricorn, Taurus.
I call to Earth,
to the fields of winter grasses and the
    deep woods,
blanketed in moss.
To the dry leaves of summers past
that signal autumn and colder nights.
To the many mysteries and secrets
    held aloft
by the jeweled tapestry of black tree
    limbs in the night sky.
To the silent trail of the stag as it weaves
    its way
through the dark of the forest,
and to Gaia, our great Mother,
who holds us all in her bountiful
    embrace.
To the fruit on your trees, Gaia,
the nourishment of your plants,
the blessing of your sacred herbs.
To sand, soil, salt, and spice.
To rock and mountain where
    we climb

to remind ourselves of our own potential,
and to vistas far and wide, landscapes
    green and brown,
arid and tropic beauty.
Be here with us tonight, element
    of earth, and let the power of
    your grounding force call us into
    present time,
reminding us of the gift of

silence and our connection to land,
    to each other,
to all forms of life.
May the delicate and precious
    balance of these four elements
    make itself known to you, now
    and always.

Amen, A'ho, So it is

— Blessing —
New Year Intention-Setting

**To summon in new energy
streams for the year ahead**

As you meditate on the year ahead, speak
these words at the first new moon of the
new year.

As you inhale, visualize your dreams and
goals for the upcoming year, and on your
exhale, let go of the past year as you repeat
the following blessing:

*I seek to align myself ever more deeply in
the year ahead
with my Creator's plan for my life,
accessing my deepest wisdom
and most authentic power.
Great Spirit, I ask for your blessing upon
my intentions.
Please offer me the strength, courage, and
resolve to pursue my dreams, even when
I am afraid or unsure of my steps.
May my efforts support the Highest Good
of all*

*and may I be in divine service to all
my kind.
I come to you, Great Spirit, for wisdom
about my path.
I seek information, insight, and vision
as I move in the world,
helping to align my efforts and actions
with my soul's purpose for incarnating in
this lifetime.
Help me correctly interpret the signs
you reveal,
and guide my hand as I aim my arrows
of hope and beauty.
I ask for the strength to move
gracefully and
purposefully toward my becoming.
May the year ahead
be blessed in every way.
And may I effortlessly attract the
resources I need
to do your will.*

Amen, A'ho, So it is

— Invocation —
Universal Support

A calling for support from the four directions to guide your journey in the year ahead

As you read these words aloud, imagine energy gathering from all directions, bringing with it resources you need to support you on your path this year. Know that you are always guided, seen, held, and nurtured by forces near and far.

I set my vision for this new year,
focusing my will and intention on the
*   dreams within my heart.*
I open my mind and spirit
to receive and allow energies to flow
that will co-create my intention in full
*   alignment with my Highest Good and*
*   the Highest Good of all beings.*
I receive support from the North,
and the elder spirits who bring me wisdom.
I receive flow from the West,

and the grandmothers who encourage
*   my trust.*
I receive strength from the South,
and elements of courage to empower me.
I receive inspiration from the East,
and fuel for the long journeys ahead.
I receive wisdom from my Creator,
the essence of all life, and I allow that
*   knowing to flow*
and move freely through me.
I root deeply into Pachamama,
trusting that she can hold me steady
*   during the storms of life.*
And I connect powerfully with Source,
attuning to universal frequencies of love.
As above, so below.
As within, so without.
I welcome universal support from
*   all directions,*
and give thanks for spirit guidance.

Amen, Aho, So it is

— Affirmation —
and Activation
Chakra

**To open, balance, and align
the human energy centers
for a year of vibrant health**

Speak these affirmations aloud while you
touch the space of each chakra with your
dominant (or writing) hand.

Begin 12 inches (30.5 cm) above your
head, at the Soul Star or Angelic Gateway.

*At the Soul Star chakra, I activate my
    connection
to the Star Systems, Star Beings, and
    angelic frequencies.
"I am vast, I am expansive, and I am timeless."
As I repeat this mantra, I activate the
    Soul Star chakra
for healing, peace, and bliss.
At the Crown chakra, I activate my
    connection to my spirit guides and to
    Source frequencies.
"I am guided, I am loved, and I am held."
As I repeat this mantra, I activate the
    Crown chakra
for soulful connection and union with God.
At the Third Eye, I activate wisdom across
    time
and am initiated as a seer of all things.*

*"I scry and seek the knowledge of my
    ancestors, channeling this wisdom to
    heal others and myself."
As I repeat this mantra, I activate the
    Third Eye chakra
for inner knowing, Source guidance,
    and precognition.
At the Throat, I activate my truth with
    conviction and clarity
and I speak my truth with conviction.
"I hear and honor my voice as I speak
    my words
but I also wield the power of conscious
    silence."
As I repeat this mantra, I activate the
    Throat chakra
and my authentic truth, embodied fully
    and freely.
At the Heart, I love and accept myself as
    I am today
and extend that gracious acceptance
    to others.
"I grow and expand every day, a model of
    love for others,
radiating compassion for all beings."
As I repeat this mantra, I activate the
    Heart chakra
for compassion, abiding love, and soulful
    connection.*

At the Solar Plexus, I am a person of
power,
stronger and more energized every day.
"I am the author of my life, writing the
words of the sacred texts of my
existence in flowing inks of love and
gratitude."
As I repeat this mantra, I activate the
Solar Plexus chakra,
and I forgive the past, for my power is in
this moment only.
At the Sacral, I am a fountain of
creative potential,
and desire flows to and from me in all
directions.
"I create life, I deliver life, I am
life itself.
I glow from within, a reflection of the
Divine."
As I repeat this mantra, I activate the
Sacral chakra
for passion, creativity, and physical
connection.

At the Root, I am safe and secure,
and I have learned that wherever I am
is home.
"I take up my space with pride and
unapologetic wisdom.
I have enough. I am enough. I know
enough."
As I repeat this mantra, I activate the
Root chakra
for stability, protection, and safety.
At the Earth Star, I am anchored in Gaia's
crystalline matrix, and I gather my
strength from the stone people.
"I receive wisdom and energy from the
crystals around me,
and through them, I attune to the cosmic
frequency of truth."
As I repeat this mantra, I activate the
Earth Star chakra,
and in doing so I align my energy to the
energy of all life.

Amen, A'ho, So it is

— Project 1 —
Intention Altar

To open a sacred container for your dreams and visions

You can use this Intention Altar to raise energy for what you desire this year. Ideally, you should represent the four cardinal elements on your new altar.

An altar designed to represent intentions of wealth, fame, or love should be placed in the south, while an altar designed to raise energy for spiritual growth, work success, or travel should be placed in the north. You can combine several intentions on one altar by placing a single item representing each intention in the corner aligning to the appropriate direction for each intention. When in doubt, follow your intuition.

continued

Gather:

- A chalice or vase of fresh flowers for water
- Bowl of palo santo, copal, or white sage for smudging
- An altar cloth or beautifully printed scarf (optional)
- A feather
- Crystals for earth
- A candle for fire
- A lighter
- Divination tools, such as a pendulum, oracle cards, tarot cards, runes, or casting stones (optional)
- A journal and pen (optional)
- Your personal power crystal or other power tool (optional)
- A statue of a deity aligned to your intention (optional)
- I also like to include an item to represent the element of love, such as a love crystal or a pink candle, which should be the anchor for all energetic work.
- I like to include a wand or two for directing energy; wands represent the element of spirit.

Look at the items you have chosen and feel your heart expand with gratitude toward them. Clear your space with the smoke of white sage, palo santo, or copal. Lay your altar cloth across your table or space. Be attentive to the details and the process here: Straighten edges, wipe off any leftover ash, and bring attention to your breath so you stay mindful.

I like to work clockwise in magic, from east to north, so I begin with the placement of my easternmost items: feather and smudging herbs. Then, I place my candles and lighter in the south. In the west I organize my divination tools, which align to the element of water, flowers, and herbs. In the north I place my journal and crystals, which represent the stone people. If you have a deity statue, you can place it in the center *or* in the direction to which the deity corresponds. Items that represent the heartspace and love can be placed in the center of your altar as well; I like to use an amethyst or a quartz heart for this purpose. Power crystals should be in the center as well, so they can draw power from the four directions. Wands can also be placed at the center of your altar, or to the east.

Once you feel satisfied with the order, balance, and beauty of your altar, smudge one more time, bringing the smoke of the herbs and resins up, over, and through all the items. Then, bow your head and bring your hands to prayer position at your heart, giving thanks for the gathering of magic before you. May it serve you well.

Amen, A'ho, So it is

— PROJECT 2 —
Law of Attraction
3D Crystalline Vision Board

To attract what you seek and engage the Hermetic Principles for creative power

By mentally connecting with an image or set of images over and over, consistently and with intention, you begin to set wheels in motion, chains of events unfolding in micro steps so small you will likely not even know things are happening until, well, they land on your doorstep! Your mind is a powerful thing. So let's put it to work by making a powerful vision board, shall we?

Select magazine clippings or printouts to create your mental collage or crystalline vision board. Include images of nature, which can represent primal and elemental energy on your board.

continued

Gather:

- A candle to burn while crafting, preferably in shades of indigo to open the Third Eye (optional)
- Essential oil to anoint your board for extra energy (optional)
- A large piece of cardboard or poster board, at least 12 × 18 inches (30 × 45 cm)
- 20 to 30 clippings of images to align to the energy of your intention
- Chip stones or crystals to make your board 3D (optional)
- Liquid cement or glue stick to adhere your images
- Palo santo, copal, or white sage for smudging

As with most sacred work, this project must begin with an intention. Remember that the ethics of intention setting require two considerations: First, your intention *must be for you alone.* We do not ethically work magic *for others,* even if our intention is to help. Second, your intention *must be in alignment with the Highest Good,* not only yours but the collective. Causing harm to others, intentionally or unintentionally, is not your right.

Set an intention for yourself and what you wish to enjoy or experience. Ask that you be able to enjoy this arrival freely, without encumbrance or fear. Allow yourself to step into this vision for a moment in your mind. How does it feel to create or receive what you desire? Fill your heart and mind with the energy of that juicy connection to your dreams.

Come up with one phrase or sentence that captures the essence of what you wish to envision into reality. Say it out loud. And then, light your candle. Anoint with a sacred perfume aligned to intuition or channeling, if you desire. And then clear off your board. Look over your clippings and chip stones or crystals, clustering them if you feel called by a theme or color and gluing them in place. Turn on some music that inspires you and let the magic unfold.

Smudge a little just because it feels good to do sacred work in a clear energetic space. Enjoy the process—don't place rules or restrictions on what you put together. Trust that a higher power is guiding your hand. Sing or laugh a little. Watch with wonder as a message emerges. When your vision board feels complete, smudge it, bless it, and hang it where you can see it. I like to blow my breath of life across my vision board each day, affirming my commitment. May yours bring what you seek in perfect time and remind you that magic is real.

Amen, A'ho, So it is

2

February

THE MONTH OF NEW AND UNIVERSAL LOVE

In February, winter's chill loosens its grasp on the land. We arrive at the midway point between winter and spring in the northern hemisphere, a time to celebrate. Much of nature is pregnant with life, which is reflected by the holiday Imbolc, February 1. *Imbolc* means "in the belly," and you are invited to think about what is gestating inside of you. Are you kindling your inner fire? Love has brought us through the cycle of conception. Now, the waiting begins. It isn't yet time to burst forth into the world with all your dreams fully materialized. Prepare as much as you can for what is coming. Turn your gaze inward, and stay there.

This month, energy streams of *self-love* and *universal love* are easily accessible. Invite them in by gently bringing your attention to your breath, speaking your full birth name out loud, and then asking self- and universal love energies to come into your heart. Imagine your heart opening wide to receive them. Welcome these energies and thank them for their presence. The blessing, invocations, and project in this chapter are designed to attract general love energies to you. Are you ready to serve as a channel and conduit of love? By choosing yes, you also welcome the inverse of love. Everything has its opposite, and like and unlike are the same. We must know both love and its opposites to understand it. On a practical level, you will experience hate, disgust, and sorrow while you welcome love. That is law.

And is why one *must* be vulnerable in love; it is the only way to really feel it. You might get terribly hurt along the way. But you might also get terribly loved. May you feel and embody both love and its opposite with grace, now and always.

Y a'ho

— BLESSING —
Valentine's Day

To invite love in all its forms

*I seek love, and I know
that love is also seeking me.
Love is the tie that binds,
the force that unites,
the frequency that heals,
and the wisdom that grounds us.
Beyond all judgment and limitation
exists a love that knows no boundaries,
a love that knows no fear or hesitation.
Today I summon and welcome this love
of force, magnitude, and creation
to enter my life and bless my soul.*

*I in turn summon and welcome this love
to pour out from within me,
so that I too become not just the recipient
but also the channel
for this divine love energy.
Love comes to me from the east,
and I welcome its breath of inspiration.
Love comes to me from the south,
and I welcome its passion.
Love comes to me from the west,
and I receive its healing.
Love comes to me from the north,
and I rest steadily in its embrace.*

Amen, A'ho, So it is

— Invocation —
Love Draw

**A calling to summon
the Twin Flame**

*I call to the winds of the four directions,
and draw them toward me.
I ask you, Great Spirit, to guide true and
    immortal love
toward my heart and home.
I seek the love of my lifetime,
and I know that because I seek it,
it is also seeking me,
for no desire is placed upon the human
    heart in vain.
The love I seek,
a partnership that nourishes me,
sustains me, honors and supports me
is the love they call
the Anam Cara, the soul's mirror,
The Twin Flame:
A beloved I shall recognize from lifetimes
    of connection,
remembering him or her across seas of
    longing and belonging.*

*Please, Great Spirit, bring this
    love to me,
so that I might spend all my days
in the sacred embrace
of the one who knows me from within
and without,
from above
and below.
Let me be still and be loved
by the one who sees me
and whom I see
with tender clarity.
I summon this love and, once found,
I vow to cherish it until my last breath.
For the Highest Good of all,
so it shall be.
"I feel the life force flowing
    through me,
and I am a healthy open channel for it
    to manifest
in human form."*

Amen, A'ho, So it is

— Invocation —
Imbolc Self-Love

A gathering of energies for wellness and self-care

The turning of season from winter to spring is a sacred occasion. Use this invocation to honor Brigid, goddess of middle winter, and invoke the element of fire in her sacred flame.

Today at middle winter, I feel a stirring.
All around me, signs of life emerge
from beneath blankets of snow and ice.
Within me, life emerges too,
and I honor the return of light,
strengthening my life force on this
*   sacred day.*

I light a candle to Brigid, goddess of the
*   eternal flame.*
I am grateful for Mother Earth and
*   her gifts.*
I invoke the radiant energy of the sun,
as I feel the days growing longer.
The sun's gentle return, the flame,
its rays spreading warmth across the land,
*   across my heart.*
I am the light. I share my light with others.
And in doing so, my light expands.
May all that I touch grow, bloom,
*   and flourish*
with love and in beauty, always.

Amen, A'ho, So it is

— Project 3 —
Love Draw Medicine Bag

To attract new love into your life

The items you gather for this project are all sacred to both Venus and Aphrodite, the Roman and Greek goddesses of love, respectively. Ideally, gather the items on Friday (Venus day), or create the medicine bag on a Friday, or do both on Friday.

Center yourself and call your energy into present time by speaking your full birth name out loud three times. Take a deep breath, enjoying the delicious inhale fully; on the exhale, release all inhibitions you may be holding toward love. Let go of fear, feelings of unworthiness, or anger about past wounds. You are setting the stage for a new love to reach you. Focus on him, focus on her. Focus on what is becoming, not what has been. The magic you work will be more potent, energized, and durable.

continued

- White sage or palo santo to cleanse and clear your space
- Selenite or quartz wand to open sacred space
- Dried hibiscus leaves
- Patchouli essential oil or dried herbs
- Rose petals
- Dried rosemary
- Balm of Gilead bud
- Dried damiana herb
- Rose quartz
- Magnetite or magnesite
- Small bowl
- Rose essential oil
- Rose geranium essential oil
- Small magnet
- A strand of your hair as an object link (optional)
- Almandine garnet, jet, hematite, or onyx to ground your energy upon closing your space
- Small organza bag in either pink, burgundy, or green

Use as many or as few of these items as you feel called to by your spirit guides. As you gather each item, gaze up to Father Sky and give thanks to Source for the blessing of its growth, its presence, and its wisdom. Once you have arranged your items, smudge them.

Open your sacred space (see page 6). Mix your herbs together with your hands, gently massaging and crushing them to release their oils and fragrance, then combine the herbs with the crystals in a small bowl. Feel the textural juxtaposition between herb and stone, enjoying the earth-based alchemies they hold and represent. Once the mixture is combined to your satisfaction and complete pleasure, pour a few drops of each essential oil over it. Allow yourself to fully delight in the union.

Place everything into the organza bag and take a deep breath. Blow your exhale, or your life force, across the bag, infusing each ingredient with your unique energetic codes and frequencies. This medicine will only be as powerful as the intention you set while creating it. Stay there: Don't doubt for a moment how powerful this work is, and how powerful you are as the magician. Allow this to be a moment whereby you simultaneously create magic and reify your own personal commitment to your life path and force.

May it be so. For it is done.

Place this Love Draw Medicine Bag upon your primary altar if you only have one, or on your love altar. Give thanks to your spirit guides and ancestors, release them, and prepare for love to come in perfect time.

Amen, A'ho, So it is

3

MARCH

THE MONTH OF EMERGING LIFE

There is something different about the months when we change season; they are periods of transformation. In March, all of nature is heavy with seeds and pregnancy. It's as if every tree is about to burst into bloom, and every expecting mother is on the edge of delivery. There is an aura of welcome anticipation to March. You just know warmer, happier days of hope and laughter are ahead once you get past the labor, the birth, the release.

But first you must get past the labor.

Nothing beautiful is born without toil. That is the lesson of childbirth. But there is beauty in the struggle. Can you see the sacred in the situations of your life? March is an invitation to find balance in your life, as it anchors the spring equinox in the northern hemisphere. Where in your life do you need to seek and discover balance? Are you aware of your light and shadow, and do you honor them equally? This month, energy streams of *integration* and *preparation* are activated. Now you are called to take the wisdom of your winter slumber and turn it into active knowing. Your spirit guides are leaning closer to you now. Will you listen to them? Nurture all these seeds of wisdom and inspiration, for in the months to come you never know which of them will bear the ripest fruit.

The quality of balance you strike in March will dictate the strength you have in summer to support your own growth. What you do this month really counts. Be mindful about your words and your time. Try to create a better 50/50 split between work and play, knowing and trusting that often "play" is devised by spirit to inspire and enhance your work. Good ideas don't come under duress. Create space for beauty.

Y A'ho

— Blessing —
and Invocation
Spring Equinox (Ostara)

**A calling to connect with
all forms of new life**

Ostara represents the reemergence
of the goddess from the underworld,
manifesting the physical rebirth of
springtime. This is a time for celebrating!
Recite the following blessing aloud to
honor this new cycle of life.

*As the Wheel of the Year turns east,
the air warms and sweetens,
and the sun dances in the sky.
The ice of winter has become a
    flowing stream,
nourishing emergent life.
I call to you, Ostara, goddess of
    the dawn,
to help my intentions grow and blossom
like your wildflowers and your fruits.*

*Bless me as I seek to cultivate my dreams
with inspired vitality.
I celebrate fertility of all kinds
and honor my existence as a sexual being,
capable of giving and sustaining life.
With each new sunrise,
Gaia finds her balance.
Masculine and feminine, united, entwined,
and I watch now
as light overtakes the darkness.
All of life reaches now
for the sky, for liberation,
for expansion and healing.
I sing the song of spring
and kindle hope in my heart.
I ask for blessings
of fertility and beauty
upon all of Gaia's children.*

Amen, A'ho, So it is

Becoming the Mother

**A calling to summon fertility
and Divine Feminine beauty**

*I feel the call,
life seeking to be born through me,
and I feel the connection to Gaia,
to the essence of the Mother
that abides in all forms of creation.*

*I celebrate fertility of all kinds,
and the potential to create,
honoring my existence as a sexual being
capable of giving and sustaining life.
I call upon Gaia, Mary, and Quan Yin
to heal, bless, and support me*

*as I become the Mother
and create a container of beauty
for a new soul to incarnate.
Teach me, divine mothers,
how to become a profound vessel
of sacred and divine fertility.
Bless the seeds within me as they
    take root
and thrive, bringing new forms of life
and creative possibility into being.
All life flows through me,
and within me,
all life is nourished.*

Amen, A'ho, So it is

— PROJECT 4 —
Spring Equinox (Ostara) Ritual

For rebirth and renewal of spirit

Ostara is an equinox, a state of natural equilibrium. It is time for you to find your equilibrium, too, and languish in energies of renewal and restoration.

Reimagine what Ostara means for you. Maybe in addition to a traditional practice, you'll purchase a brightly colored dress or plant bulbs in your garden. Whatever you do, your focus and intention are key: What new life are you birthing this year? What resources will you need to make it happen? This ritual's sacred offerings to Ostara are tangible prayers for growth, rebirth, and expansion.

continued

Gather:
- White sage or copal for smudging
- A wand to open your circle (optional; you can always use your hand instead)
- Altar covering (optional)
- A beautiful vase or mason jar
- Fresh flowers (2 or 3 bundles of a dozen each to give yourself some freedom for creativity, with stems at least 6 inches [15 cm] long)
- Crystals and materials that represent growth and fertility, such as garnet, aventurine, quartz, or coral
- A white candle, which represents life, and a blue candle, which represents open sky for expansion
- Essential oils for spring, such as lavender, ylang ylang, rose de mai, helichrysum, and rosemary

Smudge all the items you have gathered, giving thanks for their energy and what they offer to your space and to you. Clear the space energetically, burning white sage or copal and waving the smoke of the herbs around you, your space, and all your tools. Then, with your wand or right hand, open your circle of energy to create a powerful container for your ritual. Invite and welcome the Guardians of the Four Directions (see page 7). Clear the surface upon which you will place your Ostara offerings, laying down an altar covering if you want to. Then fill your vase with fresh water and flowers to represent your intention for emotional rebirth, placing a crystal inside to represent your intention for growth.

Light your candle, which represents your intention for strength and courage, and anoint with your sacred oils to represent your intention to manifest beauty in the world. Take three deep cleansing breaths, envisioning your growth, rebirth, and expansion. How will you grow this season, what will be born or reborn through you, and how will you expand your essence in the world? Enjoy the process of imagining your future into being. If it feels right to you, recite the Ostara Blessing and Invocation in this chapter aloud. Then, extinguish your candle, and with a heart full of gratitude, release the Guardians of the Four Directions from your circle, in the opposite order in which you invited them.

Wave your wand counterclockwise to release the circle of energy, imagining it scattering like tiny stars of beauty and possibility out into the matrix where each one of your visions will anchor, root, and begin to grow. Keep saying thank you. Thank you, thank you, thank you.

With your feet firmly on the floor, send any residual energy down into Gaia's belly, where it can be transmuted into usable white light.

May your growth, your rebirth, and your expansion be blessed.

Amen, A'ho, So it is

— Project 5 —
Balance Grid

To honor the dualities of equinox

Grids are energy vortexes; they are places of power and magic. Are you ready to raise energy for your dreams?

Gather:

- Palo santo, copal, or white sage for smudging
- A quartz generator, obelisk, or pyramid
- Gemstones aligned to balance: lepidolite, sodalite, blue kyanite, fluorite, sapphire, turquoise, larimar, chrysoprase, and blue opal are good options
- Herbs or flowers of balance and equalization (optional): lotus root, hydrangea, rosemary, and thyme are good options
- Double-terminated quartz point

Think of grids as *compasses*, anchoring the energies of the four cardinal directions: north for wisdom; east for new beginnings and new life; south for courage and strength; and west for emotional balance, healing, detoxification, and grief. You can make a simple grid using a generator in the center and four crystals at the quadrants; or you can "cut the quadrants" into quarters, making cross-quarters, and expand the energy, increasing the number of crystals to eight, and then sixteen, and then thirty-two. Each time you expand the circle by multiples of four, you radiate a higher frequency.

Begin by smudging the crystals. Place your generator in the center of your grid, visualizing a beam of white divine light flowing from beneath it, through it, and out toward the heavens. Then working clockwise, place stones around your generator. If you have four stones, place one at each of the cardinal directions. If you have eight, you can place two at each direction or one at each direction and each cross-quarter direction (e.g., NE, NW, SE, SW).

continued

From there, with each additional four stones, you can cross the quarters again into eighths, making a mandala design, or you can extend the limbs of a basic four-directional or eight-directional grid. Base your decision on the aesthetics of your grid *or* on the energy. Including more stones in fewer directions will empower the energy streams more directly. Add herbs or flowers as desired.

Once your grid feels complete, charge it with a double-terminated quartz point. Touch one end of your point to the generator in the center of your grid, and then touch the easternmost crystal in the center of your grid. Focus your energy and attention on your intention for building this grid, which is balance. Moving clockwise, touch the center generator and then each crystal in the grid, forming a spider's web of energy around the grid. Once you return to the center generator, stop, close your eyes, and declare that the energetic field of the grid is open. In doing so, you allow the flow of energies to begin.

If and when you decide to close the energy of this grid, open your circle, remove and bless items in a counterclockwise direction, and smudge and thank each item for its service. This is best done at a new moon or during a waning moon phase.

Great Spirit, we thank you for blessing our sacred work and honoring our need for balance at this time.

Amen, A'ho, So it is

*Are you ready to raise energy
for your dreams?*

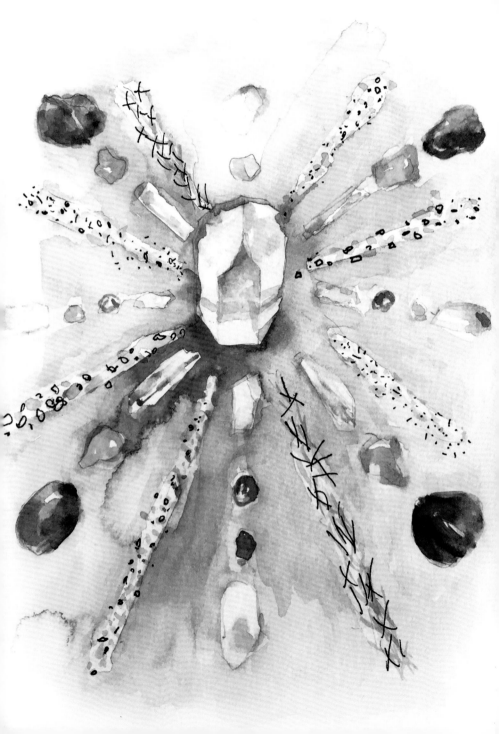

4

April

THE MONTH OF HEALING AND WELLNESS

When you open your door in April, a full symphony of nature's music awaits you. Birds are singing their songs of hope and freedom, while winds whisper through trees full of tender green leaves. The fullest display of nature's beauty awaits you, of course; the most heavily scented of her flowers have yet to spread their petals. Your heart flutters with optimism when you see life emerging and flourishing. Much that seemed to wither last winter has come back to life in new and surprising ways, reminding you not to discount the healing powers of rest and surrender. Warmer days are luring you outside. Heed that invitation; sink your feet into grass and feel your worries melt and flow down into Gaia's thick roots away from you, leaving you lighter and happier. Whatever you have carried over from winter, make one final release here and now.

April is a month of hope and a month of healing. April is the triumph of light over darkness, and it represents your own ability to persevere through intense challenges. Think about it: You have survived them all! You are a warrior, a survivor, and a teacher. You are a creator, a builder, and a steward. Honor the fullness of the expression of life that you are. How many people have you helped along this path?

This world is better because of you. Once you acknowledge that, forgive yourself, and begin to integrate your wisdom, you will finally access that healing you have waited on. Healing is an outcome of love. And the most important person who needs to love you is *you*. Use the invocations and blessing in this chapter to call in the healing you seek on physical, emotional, and spiritual levels. Living a well life is your birthright. Now is the time, and you are ready. Once you engage your faith, nothing is impossible.

Y A'ho

— Invocation —
New Moon Healing and Balance

A calling to your healing angels for healing, balance, and alignment

To begin, purify your space with white sage, and place four pieces of smoky quartz or Himalayan salt crystals (one in each corner of the room) where you will be performing your healing ceremony, as these are detoxifiers of space.

*At this new moon, I seek wellness
   and balance
of body, mind, and spirit.
I call in alignment, health, and peace.
Blood and bone, clean and pure
free of disease frequencies.
Chakras flowing, energy moving freely,*

*I channel the sacred life force.
I am aware of my access
to All Wisdom across All Time,
and my ability to unlock healing codes
at this new moon
for my wellness and Highest Good.
Source, Mother Goddess, Great Spirit,
  Father God,
I call in your breath of life of the east,
your healing waters of the west,
your sacred fires of the south,
your grounding trees of the north
to heal, transform, and protect me
   from harm.
Now and always,
may it be so.*

Amen, A'ho, So it is

— BLESSING —
Recovery and Addiction

To remove energetic bonds of addiction

*In my frailty, I have become reliant
on sources of energy
beyond my own
and I seek now to heal and transform,
free of the bonds of addiction
      and pain.
I surrender my pain and all my fear
      to Source,
so I may be held, and healed.
I recognize my humanity,
my imperfections, and my flaws.
And although I face challenges,
I love and accept myself, as I am in
      this moment.
Nothing to change, nothing to fix.
Great Spirit, I ask you to aid me in
      releasing my bonds.
I ask for your benevolent compassion.*

*I call on Archangel Michael
and Archangel Raphael to heal energies
      of addiction.
Great Spirit, please relay your divine
      guidance
so that I may know purity of mind, body,
      and spirit,
free from all negative bonds.
I no longer give power to those bonds,
for they do not serve my Highest Good.
I call back my power
and choose only what is healthy and right
      for me.
I am here, I will survive, and
I will rise above any circumstances
that deter me from my soul's true path.
I claim my wholeness and my wellness.
I claim my alignment, my place,
and my connection with God.*

Amen, A'ho, So it is

— Invocation —
Physical Wellness

**A calling to invite
physical well-being**

*Great Spirit, I thank you for this
   human lifetime
you have bestowed upon me,
for the vitality and energy that surge
   through my veins.
I thank you for my senses
~ sight, smell, touch, hearing, taste ~
and the access they offer to this
   beautiful world.
I am grateful for the unique gifts you
   have granted me,
the connections with others I know
   and love.
Thank you, thank you, thank you.*

*I ask that you continue to bless me with
   physical health,*

*strength, and peace.
Help ease the physical challenges
and discomforts of life,
so I can pursue my path
with vitality and courage.
I ask that you keep my bones strong,
   my blood pure,
my mind centered, my lungs clear,
and my heart full.
I ask for this blessing of wellness
so that I may move in the world
free of pain, worry, or discomfort
and bless others along the way,
sharing with them
what you offer so freely and graciously
   to me.
I receive my physical healing,
with gratitude.*

Amen, A'ho, So it is

— Project 6 —
Home Healing Altar

To bring health to your family

First consider what kind(s) of healing you seek to manifest: physical, emotional, spiritual, or karmic? Self-healing or healing for others? For family members or clients? Gemstone choices may change depending on your decision.

Gather:
- Smudging herbs for healing (such as palo santo or white sage)
- A crystal generator aligned to healing (hematoid quartz, clear quartz, smoky quartz, or aventurine)
- 4, 8, 12, or 16 natural or tumbled healing crystals aligned to healing need (you can choose crystals for relevant chakras or health concerns)
- A healing wand made of prehnite, aventurine, Tibetan quartz, or danburite (optional)
- A feather or smudging fan (optional)
- Healing oils and herbs (e.g., rosemary, eucalyptus, sage, thyme, basil, and aloe)
- A glass or chalice of fresh water (optional)
- A statue of a healing deity or symbol (Quan Yin or the shamanic Healing Hand, for example, optional)
- A green healing candle

Green is the color of healing, so place your altar in a green room or use a green cover. According to principles of feng shui, the ideal location for a healing altar within your home or sacred space is in the center, though a family healing altar belongs in the east.

Consider the elements as you begin to organize them. Then, smudge each item. (I also recommend smudging your entire home or sacred space before setting up this altar.) You might say, "With this smoke I clear any energies in this space that are not in service to my Highest Good or the Highest Good of those I love, and those who reside here. I call in universal White Light of love and truth to replace any energies I remove today. Amen, A'ho, So it is."

Place your crystal generator in the center of your altar, and surround it with any of the other crystal healing stones to form a mandala. Add one stone at each direction: north, south, east, and west. Or use eight or sixteen stones, cutting the quarters into cross-quarters, expanding the circle of your mandala.

continued

Place your smudging herbs or resins in the east with your wand, smudging fan, feather, or any other air-element offerings. Give thanks to the eastern guardians for their support. Next, add any healing oils to the western corner of your altar, representing water. You can also use a glass of water to represent health and hydration. Give thanks to the western guardians. If you have a healing statue of a deity, place that in the center or in the north to represent wisdom. Give thanks to the northern guardians.

Last, place your candle in the south of your altar, and give thanks to the southern guardians.

Smudge one more time. Bow your head and bring your hands to prayer position over your heart. Give thanks for the wisdom and inspiration that led to your altar's creation. May you enjoy perfect health in your home or sacred space, always.

Amen, A'ho, So it is

— Project 7 —
Flower and Herb Mandala

To raise energy for beauty, wellness, and ease

Making a mandala is a meditative exercise, one that invites simplicity, contemplation, and gratitude.

Gather:

- Palo santo, copal, or white sage for smudging
- A quartz or aventurine generator, for magnification and new growth
- Flower petals and leaves
- Tumbled gemstones or chip stones (optional)
- Tree branches (optional)
- Fruit or other edible offerings (optional)

Clarify your intention: What is your need or desire, and how might this mandala represent a gateway to a new level of awareness? Mandalas are creations of beauty and harmony but can also transport you to higher dimensions of consciousness, both through the intentional process of creating them *and* through the act of meditating upon the energy they hold.

Smudge all your gathered offerings, and yourself, focusing on your hands. Place your generator at the center of your mandala space, and place four flowers or gemstones at the cardinal directions, anchoring them with gratitude, a song, or a prayer. For example, "Great Spirit, thank you for the gifts of these crystals, flowers, fruits, branches, and leaves. I gather them in service to you and in gratitude for your greater blessings. Amen, A'ho, So it is."

Work outward from the center, adding items that lend balance and texture, color and energy, such as tree branches and fruit offerings. Then take a moment to fully appreciate its beauty and your own. Meditate, perhaps calling in wellness and ease for yourself and for our planet as well.

May you always walk the beauty path.

Amen, A'ho, So it is

5

May

THE MONTH OF PROSPERITY AND POWER

The number of fingers on each hand, the number of points on a star. The number of leaves on the cinquefoil plant, which attracts prosperity. Five is a number of completion and wealth. And in the fifth month of the year, there is a palpable energy of abundance. Work with this energy to enhance flow of financial resources ahead of the growth and harvest seasons to come.

When you think of prosperity, do you think of yourself as entitled to it or blocked from it? Does the idea of material wealth make you uncomfortable? Where do your ideas about money come from?

A river flows without thinking about how big it is, how another river might compare to it, or whether it is entitled to flow freely, expansively, and powerfully along its path. Nature models wealth to us in every way—abundance of flowers and fruits, vistas so wide and colorful your eyes can't fully take them in. Why, then, might humans feel conditioned to stay small and take up minimal space? And how does this mind-set of smallness serve us?

A sincere desire for wealth is a desire for wealth of all things for all beings at all times. When I open a portal for prosperity, that energy becomes available for the collective. I delight when I see others call in prosperity, for *all* benefit when one benefits. So ring your bell, light your candle, summon your guides, gather your crystals, bathe in salt, and let go of fear. Stake your claim to what is yours using the blessings and projects in this chapter to guide you.

Y A'ho

— Invocation —
5/5 (May 5)
Prosperity and Ease

**A calling to summon
material wealth and flow**

On the 5th of May, a power
day for money magic, read this
invocation aloud.

*I envision a life of prosperity—
a life in which my energies,
my creations, and my experiences flow
easily and freely through me.
I allow my heart to open,
and inspiration to pour through,
shining light upon channels of abundance
ready to support me beyond my dreams.
I recognize that I am,
like all of nature,*

*an abundant being
overflowing with beauty, possibility,
and infinite wisdom.
Thank you, Great Spirit, for the many gifts
you have bestowed upon me in
    this lifetime.
Help me to use them well, in service of all,
and bless me so that I can do my
    soul's work
in a state of ease and grace.
I am a being of light, child of the Divine,
and prosperity is not merely my desire
—it is my absolute birthright.
I claim my prosperity now,
and it is done.*

Amen, A'ho, So it is

Beltane

**To celebrate fire,
passion, and fertility**

*At Beltane, we honor the culmination
of spring
and the sacred union of the God
and Goddess
to bring forth new life. Our ancestors
invoked the wild, animalistic energies
of the Green Man on this day,
while dancing around the Maypole.
Repeat the following blessing aloud
to celebrate fertility and the midway point
to summer.*

*At Beltane, I ignite the sacred flame
within me,
activating my fertility, my magic.
I dance around the fire with my beloved
honoring the abundance we hold as
a union.
At this pinnacle of spring, I honor
my growth,
abundance, and sexual energy.*

*I am a being of power, maturity, passion,
and wisdom,
ripe with the fruits of Beltane.
I am manifest potential, and my creative
fire burns.
Today and always,
I ask that you help me feel and fan my
inner fire.
Today and always,
I ask that you bless me
with the continuous love of the one
whose touch I have known
for a thousand years.
May the flames, ashes, and smoke of the
Beltane fire
protect, strengthen, and inspire me
while they seduce, inspire, and
nourish me.
May the fire
that ever burns within me
also ever burn between
me and my soul's twin.*

Amen, A'ho, So it is

— PRAYER —
Sacred Box Dedication

**To bless and consecrate
sacred tools for blessings
on the season ahead**

*These tools are my offerings,
my ways into the circle.
These tools are my guides,
my escorts into the sacred.
Great Spirit and Mother Earth,
I thank you for bringing my tools to me.
I thank you for showing them to me,
and for the blessing of being their guardian.
May they hold the energy,
stir the field, keep the wisdom,
and tell me their stories.
Help them to strengthen me in times
of fear,
reassure me in times of the unknown,
and nurture me in times of great joy.*

*And when the time comes
I will surrender them back to you,
into the arms of another keeper as
you designate,
or onto another great journey.
For now, I am their keeper.
I honor their journey, and mine, the
entwined path.
No other shall use these tools
for as long as they serve me.
In your presence, I dedicate and
consecrate them
and this vessel to my work,
to the mysteries, to the great secrets
they keep
and to which I bear witness.*

Amen, A'ho, So it is

— Project 8 —
Prosperity Altar

To raise energies of wealth and financial gain

A prosperity altar is a powerful vortex that attracts energy streams of wealth and abundance. Put it in the southeast corner of your home or sacred space.

Gather:
- Palo santo, copal, or white sage for smudging
- A large quartz, citrine, or aventurine generator
- Tumbled stones aligned to prosperity: natural citrine, aventurine, hessonite garnet, yellow apatite, yellow fluorite, pyrite, emerald, jade, and green tourmaline
- A fountain or chalice of water
- Perfume or essential oils for wealth (e.g., patchouli, myrtle, basil, cinnamon, orange, and myrrh)
- 4 or 8 clear quartz or natural citrine points (not tumbled)
- Herbs associated with wealth: cinquefoil, basil, cinnamon sticks, or patchouli (optional)
- Pieces of currency
- A statue of a deity associated with wealth (optional)
- A green or gold candle
- A double-terminated quartz wand

Smudge your space and offer a prayer for prosperity. Focus on what you seek, as specifically as you can, as you set your intention.

Place your generator at the center of your altar. Bless it as a bringer of prosperity and abundance energies. Give thanks for its work. Place four tumbled stones at the corners. Use four of the same stone to create balance, or alternate stones to create visual interest. If you would like, cut the corners into cross-quarters, placing stones between the four directions. Place your chalice in the west, where it will nourish the spirits of the west who bring clearing and purification, along with your perfume or oils. Take one of your quartz or citrine points and lay it at each of the four directions as the outermost objects in your grid. Turn the points inward to ensure that the prosperity energy you're raising stays anchored in your space; by turning the points outward, you raise a more general frequency of prosperity that is allowed to extend beyond your space and bless the broader planet. Place any herbs between the crystals, adding their elemental energy. Next, add your coins in the western quadrant of your altar, as west governs water and flow. Place your statue in the center or in the eastern quadrant to

continued

welcome its energy into your space. Then place your candle at the southernmost point on your altar, and see if anything else feels called to be present.

You are ready to charge your altar (optional). Light your candle, calling in the elemental guardians of the south. As you gaze at it, imagine the prosperity you desire, and inhabit the depth of that emotion for a moment. How will you feel when you receive your abundance? Let yourself feel it now. With your right hand, extend your double-terminated quartz wand around your altar in a clockwise circle. Set the intention that energy is flowing through you and all your tools, opening a portal for connection to Source. Imagine it flowing from every corner of our universe, directly to you. Your hand will likely become warm. As you bring your wand back to its starting point, closing the circle and sealing the blessings, bow your head and bring your hands to prayer position. Give thanks for the abundance already on its way.

Amen, A'ho, So it is

— Project 9 —
Money Draw Incense

An offering to attract blessings of wealth and material success

You can use this incense every day or during rituals that welcome energies of abundance and wealth.

Gather:

- Dried herbs and flowers associated with wealth and attraction (e.g., patchouli, cinquefoil, basil, cinnamon bark, orange peel, bay, orange blossom/neroli, and catnip)
- A mortar and pestle
- Essential oils associated with wealth and attraction (same list as above)
- A quartz point or other crystal associated with wealth (e.g., aventurine, citrine, peridot, and hessonite garnet)
- A small, tight-sealing, beautiful jar

Clear your space and focus on your intention. Why are you drawing money energy? Is it for a specific purpose, or are you seeking to experience greater wealth in your life on all levels? Write your intention down or speak it aloud.

Place your herbs, one at a time, into your mortar. As you grind them, bless each and thank it. Smell the blend frequently, making sure it's pleasing. Add a few drops of essential oil and grind. Don't weight your incense down too heavily with oils; use them for their energy and as a gentle binding agent.

Place your quartz point or crystal into the incense. Place both hands over your mortar and send gratitude through your hands into the blend, asking that it bless you and anyone who works with it. For the highest good of all, may money come to you from sources seen and unseen. Store your incense in a jar. To use, place a pinch on a charcoal disk, allowing the smoke to move through your sacred space and bless you.

Amen, A'ho, So it is

6

June

THE MONTH OF BALANCE, CYCLES, AND CELEBRATIONS

We arrive at summer's door this month, ready to burst at the seams. We have been preparing for this moment for almost a year; right after harvest last year we sowed our first seeds of sacred intention for what might be possible this year. That was the first step toward this moment of our evolution, a circle of time and energy that perpetuates itself in service of our collective advancement. In short, in nature it's grow or die. There is no perpetual natural stasis. If you have been standing still too long, well, something must change. And you know it.

But this is *not* a month of sacrifice or penance. This is a month for you to begin tasting some of the sweet fruits of your desires and your hard work. Enjoy the unfolding of the season of becoming.

How will you use the summer days? Some of them should be syrupy, slow, and sweet. Some of them should be long and arduous because you are still tending your crops. Some of them should end with warm nights full of laughter and sweet toasts to tender moments. Bring new flowers from the garden into your home because they long to be near you. Each one has overcome many obstacles to bloom for you and hopes you will notice before it's too late. All of nature hopes you will notice, enjoy, stop, give thanks, take a breather, stretch out, lounge around, and yet still make sure she has what she needs, for much of her domain cannot speak to you in words. Nature speaks in flowers.

May your garden overflow with color and beauty all season long, my fellow Soulscaper.

Y A'ho

— Ceremony —
Handfasting

For a magical and ancient wedding celebration

Handfasting is an ancient Celtic tradition to bind the hands of a couple in marriage. A ribbon, traditionally of tartan, is used to signify the joining of families and clans. The following ceremony is a modern take on an ancient practice that has been used to marry couples from all faith traditions. This ceremony involves the use of four gemstones to be placed on the wedding altar in front of the betrothed couple. For earth, you can use petrified wood; for air, you can use citrine; for fire, you can use carnelian; and for water, iolite is recommended. Use your intuition when choosing alternatives.

*Beloveds, do you give this ribbon freely
    today to share your lineage with
    each other?
If so, please say,
I DO.
Today we are using four gemstones
to represent the four elements that are
present to witness your union: earth,
    air, fire, water.
Do you welcome these elementals
to witness and honor your union today?
If so, please say,
WE DO.
Handfastings can last for a year and one
    day or a lifetime. Beloveds, how long
    do you wish this handfasting to bind
    you together?
If it is a lifetime you seek together,
please say, LIFETIME.
So it is.
[Officiant wraps the fabric around
    husband/partner 1 left wrist and wife/
    partner 2 right wrist.]
Once wrists are bound,
please repeat after me:
"With this bond, I share with you my family,
my ancestral line, my blood, and all that
    I am."
It is done.
And so shall it be forever,
such that no mortal force may separate
what God has joined here.*

Amen, A'ho, So it is

— BLESSING —
Honoring the Cycles

**For elemental support
during change**

*All that begins must end,
and yet energy is neither created
nor destroyed.
Our souls and our spirits roam in eternity,
endlessly rediscovering each other.
You and I are old and young
and we have traveled many roads together.
As I say goodbye to one
who must leave this human form
    and space,
I honor the cycles and the seasons.
I am reminded of the preciousness
    of life.
I draw in the element of earth to ground
    me as I mourn,
to catch my tears, and hold my feet.*

*I draw in the element of water to move
    through me
as I allow these deepest feelings of sadness
    and loss
to come forth and flow like the rivers.
I draw in the element of fire to cleanse me
as I release and surrender what can no
    longer be.
I draw in the element of air to usher in
    winds of change.
Sadness is a precursor of joy,
and the cycles of life always prevail.
To the Earth and the Stars
we shall all one day return.
I have known you since we left the stars,
and I shall recognize you
when we reunite there together again.*

Amen, A'ho, So it is

— BLESSING —
Sacred Tool Elemental

**To summon and anchor the
four sacred directions**

Speak these words when working
with your candles, gems, perfumes,
pendulums, or other sacred tools. You
may also use these words to dedicate new
tools when you receive them or to charge
existing tools with new and refreshed
energy. You may choose to physically
turn to the directions when reading, or
simply sense the energies of the directions
as you speak the words.

*Great Spirit, Divine Creator of the
    Universe,
bless me as I use these sacred tools
to do my soul's work on this Earth
and manifest my gifts for the good
    of all.*

*Element of air, direction of east,
you breathe life into my work, inspiring me,
moving me, helping me imagine new
    beginnings.
Spirits of the east, infuse your magic into
    these tools.*

*Element of fire, direction of south,
encourage and energize my work,
motivating me and driving me,
helping me make progress as I grow.
Spirits of the south, infuse your magic into
    these tools.
Element of water, direction of west,
you flow through me and my work,
    guiding me,
directing me, helping me move effortlessly
along my path.
Spirits of the west, infuse your magic into
    these tools.
Element of earth, direction of north,
you steady me and ground my work,
holding and supporting me,
helping me stay connected to Source.
Spirits of the north, infuse your magic
    into these tools.
Thank you, Elemental Spirits,
for being present to me.
I seek to honor each of you
in the ways I manifest and mirror
your magic in my work,
my offerings, and my practice.*

Amen, A'ho, So it is

— BLESSING —
Litha (Summer Solstice)

— PROJECT 10 —
Summer Solstice Ritual

For expansion and growth to honor the sun's power

On the summer solstice, the sun is king, and your focus is on his power, his direction, and his growth. A simple, elegant, and sacred ritual to honor this day of longest sun is to drum up or down the sun.

Gather:

- Palo santo, copal, or white sage for smudging
- A representation of the sun (e.g., a carnelian or garnet ring, a sun-colored dress, or gold)
- A drum or rattle

Set an intention for this longest day. How will you use the power of this occasion? Where in your life does the sun need to shine more powerfully, casting his warm and intense gaze upon what has previously been hidden in the shadows? Which plants in the garden of your soul need the sun's warmth to grow stronger in the season of expansion ahead? Call upon Grandfather Sun to bring his brilliant illumination and bless you with an abundance of his energy. Speak your intention aloud or write it down, and take a moment to honor the integrity of your desire. Before you begin drumming, smudge your space with clearing herbs and set an intention for this longest day. Feel into what you seek, and allow yourself to experience its energy as if it is already happening in this moment. From this illuminated space, hold the solar power piece you have chosen to represent the sun in your right or masculine hand. Feel the sun's rays charging your sacred tool with power. You can choose to wear this piece while you drum or place it on the floor in front of where you will be standing. Then, when you are ready . . .

continued

Stand and face east. Bow to the east, giving thanks to the guardians of air and their gift of the breath of life. Turn south and bow, giving thanks to the guardians of fire and their gift of courage. Turn west and bow, giving thanks to the guardians of water for their gift of healing. Turn north and bow, giving thanks to the guardians of earth for their gift of protection. Turn your gaze skyward, and thank Father Sky for his blessings of faith and illumination. Last, turn your gaze earthward, and thank Pachamama for her blessings of wisdom and grounding. When you are ready, begin to drum, following your heart's own sacred rhythm and then allowing the spirit of the drum to guide you. They say one learns to drum not from a human teacher but from the spirit of the drum itself.

Drum up high, and drum down low, thanking the sun, the moon, and all the stars for their presence. Thank all of life for being present to this moment of creation. Let yourself be free in this expression of energy and transformation. Surrender a bit to your wild side. This is your time to let loose and dust off what has been covered, hidden, or obscured by fear. Drum until you feel your heartsong is complete, and then, bring your drum before you, to your heart, and bow one last time. With this final bow, your offering to the sun and your summer solstice ritual is complete.

Amen, A'ho, So it is

— PROJECT 11 —
Sacred Union Grid

To honor and protect what love has joined together

If you desire love, or if you wish to celebrate the love already present in your life, building this grid will strengthen your connection and align you to receive all love with a more open heart. Your love altar or bedroom is a natural choice for placement. According to principles of feng shui, love altars placed in the southwest of your home or sacred space attract the strongest resonant frequency, and thus will yield the best results.

continued

Gather:

- Palo santo, copal, or white sage for smudging
- A perfume or essential oil blend with notes aligned to love and protection (angelica, rose de mai, ylang ylang, vetiver, jasmine, neroli, and cedarwood are a few options)
- A pink or light green candle
- A rose quartz generator or obelisk
- Gemstones aligned to love (e.g., rhodonite, rose quartz, pink opal, pink tourmaline, rhodochrosite, morganite, prehnite, or Botswana agate)
- 4 or 8 quartz points for the outer edges of your grid, to guide the flow of energy
- Roses or other love flowers to embellish your grid (optional)
- Statue of a love deity such as Venus or Aphrodite (optional)

Center yourself, call your energy into the present by taking a few deep breaths, and focus on your intention. Are you in search of love, or do you seek to protect and strengthen an existing relationship? Write your intention down or speak it out loud, to raise the frequency of your work and begin to open a portal of energy. All magic begins with your affirmation.

Smudge the crystals and tools you have gathered. Anoint yourself and/or your stones with your love perfume, and if you desire to hold all the elements in place while you build your grid, light your candle as well. Smudging represents the element of air; anointing and placing of fresh flowers represents the element of water; your crystals represent the element of earth; and your candle represents the element of fire.

Begin by placing your rose quartz generator at the center or heartspace of your grid. From there, working clockwise to open energies, place your additional gemstones at each quarter, building from the center outward in radiating lines of energy. Once you have placed all your stones and you feel good about the balance, symmetry, and composition of your grid, place your quartz points at the outer edges of the four directions, and smudge once more. You may activate your grid by saying out loud, "With this grid, I anchor and attract energies of love and protection of my heart."

May you be blessed in love forever.

Amen, A'ho, So it is

All magic begins with your affirmation.

7 July

THE MONTH OF ETERNAL AND SOUL MATE LOVE

Love is on the menu this month, and your seat at this banquet of desire has been reserved all year long. Unlike February, which is the month of *agape*, or universal love, July is the month of *eros*—the love that sends a shiver down your spine. Yes, this is the month of soul mate connection, and energy streams of *lust, desire,* and *sexual union* are also highlighted here.

Don't get shy on me! I want to talk about desire—*your* desire—and all the things you want deep down inside. So much of your soul, your unique fingerprint, and your soul's true mission live in your innermost desires, and if my mission is to understand your soul, then I must know what is lingering in there.

Your desires are not just yours; as the famous Rumi quote suggests, *what you seek is also seeking you*. In fact, the desires of your heart were placed there as part of your *dharma*, or soul purpose for incarnating in this lifetime. You are meant to want what you want. Stop fearing your desires and start getting excited about them. View your desires as keys to your future, your purpose, and your happiness. If you start loving and supporting yourself, you will begin attracting that higher level of love toward yourself too.

Y A'ho

— Blessing —
Recommitment

For vow renewal among soul mates affirming their love

Many seasons and lifetimes
I have known your soul.
Great storms we have weathered,
pure strength we have found, and above all,
true love we have shared.
We walk hand in hand, two paths
    intertwined,
honoring how our spirits have grown
    together.
Each day, as we nurture our bond,
we are blessed with eternal love;
the energy between us is boundless,
defying space and time.
To my soul mate, my Twin Flame,
the one the Universe placed in my path
and upon my heart,
my commitment to you is as strong today
as it was then.

On this day, I repeat my sacred vows
and recommit to the promises I have made
to honor our joy, our passion,
our endless connection.
The true beauty of your soul inspires me.
I listen, fully present, to your truths,
and with an open heart I will always
    speak mine,
so that we may hear and receive each
    other.
I honor our union,
and I am blessed to share my life with you.
Day after day, growing together,
learning together in patience
    and strength.
I will love you from this day
until my last.
As long as I breathe,
you will never walk alone.

Amen, A'ho, So it is

— Invocation —
Soul Mate Attraction

To welcome a deeply intimate soul connection

*The time has come
and my heart has been readied.
With open hands and arms,
a tender heart, and deep gratitude,
I seek the touch of my beloved, my
    Anam Cara,
the one with whom my soul can rest.
Great Spirit and all of my guides,
ancestor spirits and guardian angels,
I call upon you and ask with gratitude
for you to help guide us to the place
where we will find and recognize each other.
Please connect us in perfect time,
so that we can be together
and offer us a clear path to our union,
unencumbered by obstacles.*

*Bring us to this space together and join
    our hearts
that we might spend the rest of our days
    and nights
in each other's tender embrace.
I prepare my mind, body, and spirit
to receive love in the presence of the one
whose being completes my own.
I surrender to a love so deep
it will take this lifetime and beyond
just to explore it fully.
For the Highest Good of both parties
    and all kind,
I seek this love
and even before it arrives,
I am grateful for its presence.*

Amen, A'ho, So it is

— Project 12 —
Bedroom Altar

For passionate connection with your beloved

July brings energy of intense passion and eternal love, so why not harness those energies in the bedroom? Choose items that will not disturb your natural sleep cycles.

Gather your items during a waxing or full moon phase. Smudge your tools, your bedroom, and yourself, and release any energies that are not in alignment to your deepest soul mate connection. If you have had disagreements or arguments in the bedroom, pay special attention to those areas when you smudge.

continued

Gather:

- Palo santo, copal, or white sage for smudging
- Altar covering (optional)
- A gemstone sphere that represents passion and desire (e.g., orange calcite, green garnet, vesuvianite, sunstone, or peach moonstone)
- A feather or wand to represent air energy (optional)
- An orange candle
- A perfume or massage oil blend made with oils aligned to love and passion (e.g., ginger, rose de mai, damiana, ylang ylang, patchouli, pink lotus, and jasmine)
- Crystals aligned to your passion
- Rose petals (fresh or dried, optional)
- Damiana herb (fresh or dried, optional)
- Small bowl for holding passion herbs (optional)
- A photograph of you and your beloved in a beautiful frame
- Fresh flowers or a live plant (optional)

Choose a location for your bedroom altar. The southwest corner brings love and partnership, while the westernmost corner represents love and family—optimal placement if you are trying to conceive. Clear the location. Place an altar cover down (if desired) and set your gemstone sphere in the center or heartspace of your altar. To the east, place your smudging herbs, feather, and/or wand; to the south, place your candle. To the west, place your oils or perfume and fresh flowers or live plant; to the north, place any other crystals aligned to passion and desire as well as your dish of herbs, if you choose to include them. Place the photograph behind your sphere, and then say a prayer for peaceful and meaningful connection with your beloved. The Recommitment Blessing and Soul Mate Attraction Invocation from this chapter are ideal options, whether you are in a relationship now or seeking to attract one.

Close your eyes, place your hands on your sphere, and call into your mind an image of you and your beloved enjoying your relationship more than you ever have before. See yourself and feel yourself so in love that your entire body tingles with excitement and anticipation. Infuse that energy into the sphere, imagining it full of sweet love and explicit desire. Now, open your eyes, release the sphere, and say thank you to your passion guides.

And then, go enjoy your newly energized passion space with a night of soulful lovemaking. Cheers to your passion, dear one!

Amen, A'ho, So it is

— Project 13 —
Inner Fire Perfume

For Sacral chakra energy to enhance desire

Essential oils are living, vibrational essences of plant teachers, and they hold wisdom, power, and potential. This project will help you craft a new sacred perfume to honor the inner fire during this month of divine passion.

Use your intuition to choose essential oils for this perfume. At right are my suggested essential oil and carrier oil options. You will also need a 1-ounce (28 g) container, and I recommend adding a tiny chip stone or quartz point to the bottle to bring crystal energy.

continued

Essential oils and absolutes aligned to the inner fire of desire and creation (Sacral chakra or Svadhisthana):

- Cinnamon
- Damiana
- Ginger
- Jasmine
- Neroli
- Opoponax
- Patchouli
- Pink peppercorn
- Rose de mai
- Styrax
- Ylang ylang

Carrier oils for high-vibrational perfume making:

- Avocado
- Fractionated coconut
- Hemp
- Jojoba

- Small clear glass bottle
- Perfume vessel

Gather the oils that call to you, either from the lists on page 81 or from your own experience. Then, choose a small clear glass bottle for blending before decanting into your perfume vessel. Say a prayer and invite elemental guardians and spirit allies from the south to be present with you for this work, because they govern the enchanted realms of desire.

Begin with your essential oils and absolutes; you will add your carrier oil after. Start with the two essential oils that call most strongly to you when you think of your inner fire, your sexiest self, your ultimate seduction. Blend them, a few drops at a time. Stop, swirl, and smell. Do you like their rhythm, their partnership? Does it resonate? And most important,

does it require something more? If not, stop here. If something more *is* needed, choose the next option that speaks to you. First smell the opened bottle next to your blend to test the partnership. If you like it, add a little, a few drops at a time. Stop, swirl, and smell. Inhale, exhale. Relax and allow yourself to be with the unfolding essence of this perfume. Is it speaking to you? What secrets does it contain?

Continue testing and adding until the final blend has revealed itself to you. Place your crystal into your perfume bottle (optional), and add your blend, slowly, enjoying the view and the scent. Allow yourself to be seduced by it.

Amen, A'ho, So it is

8

August

THE MONTH OF THE SHIFT TOWARD DARKNESS

In August, we begin the long farewell to summer, not because seasons are changing but because the fruit is already beginning to ripen on the vine and the harvest is not just a single gathering of crops, but a series of long goodbyes to nature.

August is the beginning of the turn toward darkness.

It is a bittersweet farewell, for most of our growth potential of the year has already been realized. Our main achievements of the year are behind us. For some, this realization is a source of sadness; for others, this surrender opens a gateway to abundance and other blessings, including gratitude. We learn to appreciate what we have.

Leave an offering behind, a gesture of thanks and a gesture of faith for what has yet to unfold. Offerings are your way of contacting Pachamama, the Great Mother, and letting her know that you are working with her medicine. At Lammastide, on August 1, we celebrate the early harvests of the season—the wheat, the citrus, the flowers. Give back something small in return: a song that you sing, a sprig of dried herbs, a small gemstone, or another organic treasure. Some like to burn herbs and smudge while they gather their crops. Others prefer to bake bread to honor First Harvest. However you celebrate, remember that this is a time of *reflection* and *appreciation*, not only for what has come to pass but also for what has been lost, for both have taught you valuable lessons and advanced you on your soul's developmental path.

All harvests are good harvests through such a lens.

Y A'ho

— BLESSING —
Lammas

To usher in First Harvest and the gift of wheat

Lammas represents the culmination of the summer season and the celebration of a bountiful harvest. Repeat the following blessing aloud to honor the abundance of summer.

At First Harvest, I give thanks
for the abundance I have cultivated
and received in this first half of the year.
These crops, gifts from Gaia our Mother,
come after seasons of sacred intention.
I dive deeply to the Earth within,
to the soil of my spirit,
and there I gather the fruits
of what I planted this spring.
I gather these early crops,
honoring also those crops
that were not strong enough to survive.
For they have also given of their beauty,
and blessed me with lessons of loss.
I prepare for the rest of the harvest now,
softening into fall and resting more
in the sunset of the year.
I use hematite and obsidian
to ground and surrender
my trust in the Universe.
I am safe, I am held, I am secure.
My efforts rewarded, I honor the Earth.
As the Great Wheel hints at summer's end,
I prepare my spirit for feast and rest.
Well-tended seeds, sown with care,
will yield a good harvest for all.
So shall it be.

Amen, A'ho, So it is

— Project 14 —
Despacho Ritual to Pachamama

For blessings in the harvest season ahead

A *despacho* is a profoundly meaningful prayer offering traditionally practiced by Q'ero shaman in the Andes Mountains of Peru, where the Apu spirits of the local mountains continue to guide ritual and ceremonial practices. A despacho offering can be made anywhere, and at any time, and should include items you have at your disposal; what matters most is the intention beyond your offering, not the specific items you include, though traditionally you should include something sweet and leaves that have been infused with your breath or life force, the two sweetest medicines in a despacho bundle. The purpose of a bundle is to give thanks to Gaia, to Pachamama, to our great Earth Mother for the bounty she provides without asking for much in return. Think of it as Gaia's Mother's Day gift. To the Q'ero shaman, despacho is one tool to enact *ayni*, or cosmic balance, creating equity in the exchange between Pachamama and her children. This is your chance to give back in a good way for all you receive every day.

Gather:

- Palo santo, copal, or white sage for smudging
- A piece of paper or a paper bag, unfolded, upon which to create your mandala of offerings
- Leaves from local trees to represent prayers (Traditionally, coca leaves from the Amazon would be used here, but barring access to those, please choose leaves with meaning to you from your local garden or forest.)
- Organic items to represent gifts (Grains, sweets, shells, gemstones, flowers, and herbs are beautiful examples.)
- String to tie your despacho
- Firepit or other source if you wish to burn your despacho in the traditional way (An alternative will be discussed.)

continued

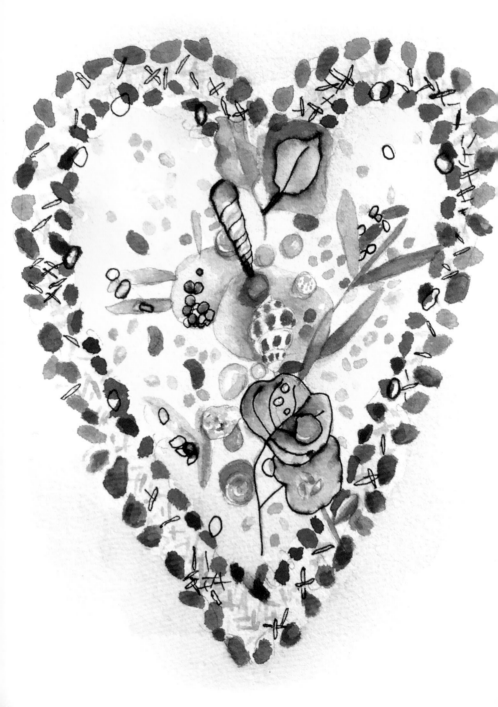

You can do your despacho ritual alone or in a small group—either way is powerful. In a group setting, remember that you are always working not only with your unique intentions and energy but with the energy and intentions of the collective as well. All will need to be included, represented, and the process shared.

When you are ready, smudge your despacho items with smoke of copal, sage, or palo santo. Place your piece of paper on your altar. Then, take a bundle of your leaves and wrap them in your hands; bring them to your mouth and blow your breath of spirit across them, using your breath as a prayer offering. Take a moment to center yourself here and focus on your intention, your prayers, and your gratitude. This is your time with your cosmic mother. Spend it wisely and in a way that you will enjoy. Next, on top of your layer of leaf prayers, place the gifts you have brought—sweets, crystals, flowers, found feathers, or stones—and position them in a pleasing way, focusing on symmetry and balance. Then, once all your gifts are positioned and you have given thanks once more, bring the edges of your paper together and fold them over the top, carefully wrapping the despacho without turning it over so you do not spill the offerings inside or disrupt their order.

Once your bundle is neatly folded and closed, tie it with your string and say a final prayer as you do, reminding Pachamama and your earth guides that this is your sacred expression of divine gratitude. At this point in a traditional despacho ceremony, the shaman would take the bundle and burn it privately. You may choose to burn or bury your bundle, because depending on the land where you live, fire may not be legal or advisable.

However you give this bundle back to Pachamama, do so with loving intention. May you be blessed for this expression of gratitude in ways that advance your progress on your spiritual path.

Amen, A'ho, So it is

———

*It is almost time to say goodbye
to nature's bounty.*

*By expressing your gratitude for one
of your blessings in a ceremonial
way, you will invite more to follow.*

———

— Project 15 —
Lammas Ritual

To usher in First Harvest and the gift of wheat

At Lammas, we give thanks for the early harvests. We get to taste the fruit of our labor, but the season of growth is now behind us. It is almost time to say goodbye to nature's bounty. For this ritual, choose one of your early soul harvests or personal victories of this year to celebrate. By expressing your gratitude for one of your blessings in a ceremonial way, you will invite more to follow.

Gather:

- Palo santo, copal, or white sage for smudging
- A white candle for gratitude or a golden candle for harvest
- An item representing one of your accomplishments already realized this year
- A crystal to bless to carry as a reminder of your future harvests and seeds of crops yet to come
- An offering to bury for blessings upon your remaining harvests

Smudge yourself and the items you have gathered. As you do, bring your attention to this moment and sit with the energy of First Harvest. The growth cycles of this year are complete. Do you feel a sense of excitement for the harvests ahead of you, or a sense of sadness and longing for what can no longer travel with you? To harvest well, one must both create something that survives and grieve the crops that did not make it. What could you have done more diligently this year to ensure strong growth of crops that withered? What did you do well to ensure that those that survived will bear strong fruit? Both the gain and the loss are your teachers.

Light your candle and turn your body to face south, which is the direction of summer and high growth. Greet the guardians of this direction, and hold the item you have chosen to represent your personal first harvest. Hold it high above your head, feeling the sun's warm gaze upon it, and allow energy to flow from your energy field through your chakras through your talisman; then, pass your talisman over the flame of your candle two times—first to express your gratitude and second to set your intention

continued

for additional blessings. Next, take the crystal you have chosen to bless and pass it over the flame of your candle, calling in a strong harvest for yourself and your relations. Take your offering in your hand and pass it over the flame of the candle. Extinguish your candle. Bury your offering in the west of your garden, to symbolically bless the remainder of your crops for this season. Place the crystal for future harvests in the east of your garden (burying it or laying it on top of the soil) to represent future growth. Finally, place the talisman representing your first harvest on your primary altar, a symbol of your potential to manifest your desires in alignment with your soul purpose.

Turn facing south, bow, and bring your hands to prayer position over your heart.

Amen, A'ho, So it is

9

September

THE MONTH OF THE HARVEST

September is a month you can feel before it arrives; there's a crispness to the warm air that signals autumn's arrival. Long summer nights grow slightly shorter, and leaves on trees glow in shades of honey and amber at sunset. Nature is coming close to finding her own personal balance and harmony as the second annual equinox approaches.

The Jewish year is ending, and a new year begins this month as we celebrate Rosh Hashanah. Mabon, the Celtic name for the fall equinox, is celebrated this month as well. Mabon is the second of three Celtic harvests—Lammas, Mabon, and Samhain, which comes next month. Mabon is the heavy harvest, while Samhain is the harvest of the dead and what is left behind from this month's efforts. At Samhain we make sure the vines are clean and prepared for winter rest.

Although this month's energies of *completion* and *release* bring our attention inward for reflection, contemplation, and connection with Source, now is also the time to plan for next year's crops. There can be no delay. While this harvest is fresh in your mind, think about what worked well this year and what did not. What could you have done to ensure stronger growth? Or maybe this year's harvests were beyond your expectations. What can you do now to ensure that next year will be equally successful? Did you enjoy the process of growth this year? What can you do to make the process more enjoyable?

The end of one precious cycle begins the next. May all your harvest celebrations be blessed.

Y A'ho

— Prayer —
and Invocation
Rosh Hashanah New Year

To honor the Jewish New Year

Rosh Hashanah is the Jewish New Year,
which is honored at the new moon each
September. Rosh Hashanah celebrates
the creation of the first humans on Earth.
Repeat the following blessing aloud to
honor the Days of Awe and the past year
of your life.

On this anniversary of the creation of
*   Adam and Eve,*
I celebrate the Jewish New Year.
At this time I welcome the Days of Awe,
and I reflect on the past year.
Now is a time of interpersonal repentance.
I seek out the souls who need to hear
*   my apologies*
to make amends for past transgressions.
I account for my actions,
and I apologize if I have hurt others.
At this sacred time,

I center and connect with my traditions.
The meal, the prayers,
the sounding of the shofar,
and the resolutions set are all
*   sacred expressions*
of gratitude and renewal.
I channel the energies of rebirth,
imagining new possibilities for the
*   year ahead.*
I look to what I have created,
and give thanks for my prosperity.
I view the world with new eyes,
at the start of this blessed new year,
approaching life with compassionate
*   thought and intention.*
I embark on the year before me,
restored and full of optimism.
May all be inscribed and sealed for a
*   good year*
that blesses me and all those I love.

Amen, A'ho, So it is

— Blessing —
and Invocation
Fall Equinox (Mabon)

A calling to celebrate
your soul's harvest

*We turn to the west today, and Mother
Ocean says yes.
Her waves crash upon the shore and
she is ready
to receive you and take from you all the
burdens you shall no longer carry into
the seasons of acceptance and rest.
We turn to the west today and Mother
Ocean says now.
Her waters still at midday as Father Sun
casts his beams of light upon her and
caresses her like a tender lover.
She is ready to teach you how to be
still and receive so that you hear
the messages of your elders now as
the veil thins.
We turn to the west today and Mother
Ocean says come.
Her deep blue majesty is an open invitation
to create better flow in your life. She
holds the key to creation, manifestation,
your rebirth.*

*And she can offer you the path, the
lightness of being, the deep permission
to just be now.
Your work of the year is done.
We turn to the west today and Mother
Ocean says let go.
Her vast expanse and power can hold the
things that weigh you down
and your worries can sink to her bottom,
float to her edges
while you experience her embrace.
She sees your fear and she washes it away
so that you can live in pure radiant
joy and peace.
Mother Ocean has been waiting for you.
The guardians and gatekeepers of the west
greet you today with open arms.
Yes, now, come, let go. Your work is
done.
So the season of balance, acceptance,
stillness, and release begins.*

Amen, A'ho, So it is

———

You are not just light or just shadow. Those are easy answers. You are all of it, and more.

———

— PROJECT 16 —
Fall Equinox (Mabon) Ritual

For good harvests and rewards ahead

For this Mabon, or second harvest, ritual, we are going to balance the scales and mirror nature's own division of light and shadow, which strike perfect balance on the two equinoxes each year.

Gather:

- One white or cream candle to represent your light harvest
- A gemstone to represent your light (e.g., selenite, scolecite, clear calcite, quartz, or petalite)
- Palo santo, copal, or white sage for smudging
- One burgundy or black candle to represent your dark harvest
- A gemstone to represent your shadow (e.g., black tourmaline, jet, golden sheen obsidian, or aegirine)
- A perfume or essential oil blend to integrate your light and shadow aspects

As you gather your Mabon tools, divide them into two sides: light tools and shadow tools. For the first part of this ritual, you will want to keep them separate; later in the ritual, you will be guided to mingle them, acknowledging the intimate dance of light and shadow.

Smudge the items you have gathered, and on the left, or *yin*, side of your altar, place your burgundy or black candle, your perfume or essential oils, and your gems that represent shadow. On the right (masculine), or *yang*, side, place your white or cream candle, your gems that represent light, and your smudging herbs. Take a deep cleansing breath and acknowledge on an energetic level that all these tools represent parts of you that need to be integrated into one dynamic whole expression. When you are ready, call upon your spirit guides to help you discern which items on the light side of your altar are ready to be moved to the shadow side, and vice versa. Is your light candle ready to glow upon your shadow stones, or vice versa? As you step forward in wisdom to move items on your altar as called by Spirit, enjoy the liberation that comes from blurring boundaries. You are not just light or just shadow.

continued

Those are easy answers. You are all of it, and more. You are the slippage between the categories we believe are fixed. You are the exception to *all the rules*. And that is why your magic is undeniable and indefinable.

Once you begin to mix the sides, keep going. In the amalgam, your peace and your deeper purpose reside. Move the stones, the candles, the offerings. When a new balance has been struck, step back and take a closer look at the alchemy of light and shadow, the balance between the hemispheres of awareness. What lessons have been unearthed here for yourself? Take a moment here to breathe, connect, center, and receive messages from your guides. Finally, bring your hands to prayer position over your heart and give thanks for what you have learned. This is the hour of balance, and here you are, in the center of All, right where you need to be. Welcome this moment. Cheers to your balance, your integration, and your health.

Amen, A'ho, So it is

— Project 17 —
Honey Blessing Jar

For sweet blessings and seeding of intentions for next year's harvest

Honey jars are old magic, with roots in ancient tradition where the use of honey in sacred work is thought to attract sweet blessings of affirmation. If you wish to attract new people, experiences, emotions, or energies into your life, then it is time to craft a honey blessing jar. And the harvest season is the perfect time to call in sweet blessings upon the seeds you are planting now for next year's crops.

Gather:

- White sage, copal, or palo santo for smudging
- A 2- or 4-ounce (60 or 120 ml) glass jar with lid
- Gemstones or chip stones aligned to your intention(s)
- 1 to 2 ounces (28 to 56 g) of herbs or flowers aligned to your intention(s)
- Honey or agave
- 2 or 3 slips of paper upon which to write your seeds of intention for next year
- A pen to write with
- Ribbons and crystals to adorn the outside of your jar (optional)
- Small beeswax candle (or vegan alternative) to melt over your jar

Think carefully about the two or three goals you have for next year. They can be vague or specific. Do you have plans for a new career? Maybe you are expanding your family, moving into a new phase with children getting older, or your aging parents require more assistance. What crops are you planting next year that are just for you?

Once you have identified two or three seeds of intention, smudge your crafting space and your supplies. Exhale deeply into your jar, infusing it with your personal life force. Center yourself, and keep your focus on your crops as you create your jar; the more focused your attention is now, the more likely your intentions will be manifest in the year ahead. There is a causal energetic relationship between your thoughts and your reality.

Begin adding items to your jar, one at a time, using your intuition. Maybe you are called first to place a quartz point or an herbal offering in the jar to set the space and magnify the ingredients you add next. With each crystal, each herb, each flower, say a blessing or prayer of gratitude as you add it: "Great Spirit, thank you for the gift and presence of this gemstone, this herb. Please allow its energy to bless my honey jar with power and love. Amen, A'ho, So it is." Once your herbs and stones

are in place, about halfway full in the jar, add honey or agave to the top, and then write on your slips of paper the two or three crops you wish to bless for next year. Try to limit yourself to one sentence for each, or even just a few words. Economy of expression is the art of the wise. Once you have expressed your intentions, fold each slip of paper into thirds and place it in your jar. Push each piece down until it is covered in honey. Then, seal your jar and adorn as desired with ribbons and crystals. Do you feel the completion of this work already? It is a profound exercise in faith, trust, and hope. It is belief in things unseen, forces at work that are not visible to your human eyes.

Place your small beeswax candle on top of your jar. You might melt a drop of wax on top of the sealed jar and then place your candle on the melted wax to attach it securely, as you will want to let the candle burn down and over the top of your jar, sealing it completely in beeswax. Once the wax has covered your seal, your intentions are set, and you can place your honey jar in a dark cabinet for as long as you wish—at least until your intentions come to pass. You can open your jar and add new intentions throughout the winter if you feel called, or simply stay with the intentions as you have expressed them here. You have been well guided, so you

continued

can trust your instincts. Nothing happens by accident, not even intentions. All desires you experienced have been placed on your heart for a reason. May yours come to pass in perfect time and full alignment with your purpose.

Amen, A'ho, So it is

The harvest season is the perfect time to call in sweet blessings upon the seeds you are planting now for next year's crops.

10 OctoBer

THE MONTH OF THE DEAD

During October, the veil between the realms of the living and the dead grows thin. It's the best time to contact the spirit world. October 31 is known as Halloween in the West, but Halloween has its roots in Celtic lore. In ancient times, October 31 was celebrated as Samhain, which means "summer's end" in Gaelic. On Samhain, which was also the night before the Celtic New Year, the ghosts of ancestors could be easily contacted for divination and guidance. Celtic and Druid priests took advantage of spirit proximity during this time and made predictions for the year ahead.

Today, many magical practitioners engage in divination on Samhain night. Samhain is considered a pagan high holiday and is honored in most earth-based traditions as the new year. Candles are lit to bring balance to the darkness, not only in pagan practice but in Hindu tradition as well. Diwali, the Hindu festival of lights, is celebrated at the October new moon and celebrates the triumph of good over evil. No matter the tradition or practice, October's magical past is anchored in the battle between light and darkness, echoed in different forms and manifestations around the world.

How will you honor the duality of light and shadow this month? Perhaps you will perform an energetic clearing of your home. Maybe you will light fragrant and colorful candles to call in Lakshmi's blessings of prosperity. Or maybe you will arrange a beautiful altar to honor your ancestors. However you celebrate, may you and your loved ones be blessed not only by your connection to each other but also by your memories of the past and your ancestral roots. Those roots are your deepest form of protection, peace, and prosperity.

Y A'ho

— PRAYER —
Entity Removal

To clear your home or sacred space and bring blessings

Place your candle on a flat surface and surround it with stones in a circle. Then, light sage and guide the smoke to each of the four directions. Speak these words out loud as you smudge.

Great Spirit, with your support and
*   blessing,*
I ask that any spirits in this place
that are not here for the Highest Good
*   of myself*
and my loved ones
be gently removed from this space.
Send them back to their source,
*   Great Spirit,*

and close any portals to my home or
*   sacred space*
that have been left open without
*   my awareness.*
In their place, please send angels
and divine beings of light
to gather and surround us.
Let us feel your light, your love,
and your peace always.
Please dispense your blessings,
Great Spirit, upon the spirits who
*   must leave.*
May they find their way
back to your loving white light of truth,
where they can be transformed
and, at last, find rest.

Amen, A'ho, So it is

— Blessing —
Diwali

**To honor the victory of
light over darkness**

Diwali, of Sanskrit origin, means
"light" or "lamp." This ancient Hindu
festival celebrated annually at the
October new moon is one of the most
important of sacred days, known as
the biggest, brightest, and happiest
of Hindu celebrations. Repeat the
following blessing aloud to celebrate
light's triumph over darkness.

On this new moon,
we remember light's victory over darkness.
Diyas glow like treasures,
thunderous sounds boom triumphantly,
illuminating the night with color and
*   sound.*
Now is the time to delight in celebration.
Lakshmi, I honor you on this day.
Thank you for blessing us with your
*   abundance.*

I vow to be a channel of clarity
worthy of your prosperity.
I revel in pure joy,
experiencing each moment as an
*   infinite expanse.*
I am present with my beloveds,
and give thanks for all my relations.
I release any fear or worry with laughter
*   and dance*
and share in the spirit of generosity.
While I celebrate wealth and abundance,
*   I look deeper still.*
The true richness of life
lies in empowering hope over despair.
I celebrate new beginnings and set
*   intentions.*
Light, love, and gratitude are the origins
*   of lasting happiness.*
I banish darkness from my life and rejoice
*   in the light.*
May the light always prevail.

Amen, A'ho, So it is

— BLESSING —
Protection

To keep safe all that you love

When you feel afraid, remember that
you have guides and guardian spirits all
around you. Their job is to protect you
and keep you safe. Use this blessing to
summon them. They always come when
you call.

*Guides, Elders, Guardian Angels and
Spirits,
come close to me in this season of shadow.
Circle around me and grant me the favor
of your protection.
Help me to feel safe, secure, and held in
my life.
Surround me and mine with a sphere
of white light,*

*and make me and mine invisible
to anyone who would do us harm.
Pave my path, guides and Great Spirit,
with ease and care.
Help me to know I am never alone.
Place people in my path
who can support me in the physical world.
Strengthen and heal my body and mind,
so that I can face my life with confidence
and courage.
And at night when I rest, grant me
sweet dreams
of joy and peace.
Surround me with love.
Fill my heart with your presence.
Thank you for the gift of this safety.*

Amen, A'ho, So it is

— Blessing —
and Invocation
Samhain

To honor the presence and wisdom of our ancestors

Samhain is a great parting of the veil between the living and the dead. Use this blessing to open the portal for greater access to your ancestors and spirit guides.

Tonight we remember those
who lived and died before us.
Those who have crossed the veil.
Those who are no longer with us.
We remember you.
I call first to the north,
where the Earth is silent and dark.
Spirits of the Earth, we welcome you,
knowing it is to you that we shall one
*   day return.*
I call to the east, land of new beginnings,
the place where breath begins.

Spirits of Air, we call upon you,
knowing you carry our life force.
I call to the south, source of light
that guides us through the cycles of life.
Spirits of Fire, we welcome you,
knowing you have the capacity to create
*   and rebirth.*
I call to the west, a place of underground
*   rivers,*
where the sea is a never-ending, rolling tide.
Spirits of Water, we welcome you,
knowing you will carry us gracefully
across the ebb and flow of this life.
The Wheel of the Year turns once more,
and we cycle into darkness.
At the end of that darkness comes light.
And when it arrives, we will celebrate
*   once more.*

Amen, A'ho, So it is

— Project 18 —
Ancestral Altar

To work with ancestors who have crossed into healed space

It is believed that the dead know when you place a photograph of them on an altar or sacred space and that doing so keeps their memory and their energy alive. At Samhain, the veil between the living and the dead is thin and permeable. Invite the spirits of your loved ones who have crossed into healed space to join you as you create this altar.

continued

Gather:

- Palo santo, copal, or white sage for smudging
- Altar covering (optional)
- Candles and/or tealights in shades of black, burgundy, and pink to represent love and mourning
- Dried flowers or herbs to scatter (Marigolds are traditional, but roses are lovely too.)
- Gemstones aligned to the season (e.g., tourmaline, jet, onyx, petrified wood, or amber)
- Crystal skull(s)
- Items sacred to or loved by your ancestors (e.g., candy, special foods, mementos, or jewelry)
- Small frames with photos of loved ones who have crossed

Choose where you will build your *ofrenda*, or altar of offerings to your ancestors. Select an open space where your family or guests will see it. Gather your items and smudge them well. Some choose to use an altar cover or arrange items at different heights, so think about organization and artful display as you begin placing pieces on your altar.

Place candles in the south of your altar to represent ancestral courage and strength, which you will draw upon each time you visit at this altar. Dried flowers can be scattered across your altar or placed in the east, as they represent the passage of life and the renewal of cycles. Your gemstones, including your crystal skulls, should be placed to the north, which represents the mineral kingdom. And special foods, mementos, candy, or jewelry should be placed in the west, which represents transformation and healing. Try to find open spots where your photographs can rest. Space them evenly apart, taking care to create balance and symmetry.

Once you are satisfied with your altar, it is time to dedicate it. Close your eyes, bring your hands to prayer position over your heart, and focus your thoughts on the ancestors you are choosing to honor in this space. Allow your heart to swell with love and gratitude for them. Then, speak these words aloud: "Ancestors, you are welcome here and your wisdom is appreciated. I have created this space to commune and connect with you, and for you to do the same. May we continue to be joined in our hearts across space and time, always." Enjoy the process of sharing sacred space with your loved ones once again.

Amen, A'ho, So it is

— Project 19 —
Protection Bundle

**To hold protective energies
and keep you safe in
the darker season**

In October, spirit activity increases,
and so too does our need for psychic and
auric protection. All energy is composed
of both light and shadow aspects; to
manage both well requires thoughtful
preparation and mindful use of tools.
Think of this bundle as a traveling, mini
protection altar.

Gather:

- White sage, copal, or palo santo for
  smudging
- A 4-inch (10 cm) square of fabric
- Protection perfume or essential oil
  blend (optional)
- Herbs and resins of protection (e.g.,
  angelica, dragon's blood, osha root,
  clove, juniper, myrrh, and rosemary)
- Crystals for protection (e.g., black
  tourmaline, petalite, aegirine, jet, onyx,
  and petrified wood)
- Twine or ribbon
- A protective charm or talisman
  (optional)

If you make your bundle at the new
moon, you can use it to set intentions for
protection in your life; if you craft your
bundle at the full moon, you can use it
to amplify protection for yourself, your
home, or anywhere you decide to keep
your bundle. The closer you craft to the
full moon, the more potent the energy
will be. It is not recommended to craft at
a waxing moon unless you are releasing
energy or using your bundle to mourn
or let go of something you no longer wish
to carry.

Center yourself, bring your attention
to your breath, and examine the items
you have gathered for your protection
bundle. Smudge them. Hold your square
of fabric in your hands. Smooth out the
fabric, and then place a drop of your
anointing oil or perfume blend at each of
the four corners. You are creating a strong
container for the herbs and crystals. Add
your herbs, a pinch at a time, to the center
of your bundle, blessing and giving thanks
for the energies of each. Choose one or
two crystals you wish to include, and place
those also in the center of your bundle.
If you have any other items you wish to
place inside, do that now. To make your
bundle even and attractive, bring the two

continued

sides of the fabric over and fold, then do the same with the top and bottom. You should end up with a small rectangular package.

Wrap your ribbon over the top, being careful not to spill the ingredients inside. Then wrap it under, turning the bundle over, and secure it. Bring the ends around to the front, and if desired, add your charm or talisman to one end of the string. Finally, tie the ends once more in a bow or knot. Blow your breath across the finished bundle, and then take it between your hands, bringing your hands to prayer position over your heart. Connect deeply with the energy of these offerings that have been chosen to protect and care for you. Give thanks for this new tool and the safety you will feel as you work with it.

Amen, A'ho, So it is

11 November

THE MONTH OF GRATITUDE

Gratitude is a typical theme for November; in North America, families gather this month to celebrate Thanksgiving and the abundance in their lives. But gratitude is important this time of year not just because of the holiday season; gratitude should naturally follow the season of harvest. Nature has just bestowed upon you her most infinite blessings—another year of health and home, family and loved ones surrounding you, strong crops, and food to eat. To live a ceremonial life means taking the time to pause, reflect, and give thanks before turning inward for rest in the winter months. When you cook a meal using the freshly harvested fruits, vegetables, and grains you (or others) have grown, you honor the contributions of all who worked hard to bring those offering to your table. Before you consume your Thanksgiving meal, offer a blessing like the one in this chapter as a means of expressing your appreciation and being mindful of the cycles of life.

What are *you* most grateful for this year? You can express gratitude not only for the beauty in your life, but for the challenges as well. Everything is a teacher.

Gratitude begins the cycle of abundance in your life, so once you say thank you for everything in it, get ready for the universe to bless you in big ways! That is why this month you will also enjoy an 11/11 Law of Attraction ritual you can complete on November 11 to attract synchronicity. By getting into energetic alignment with your desires, you can manifest them far more easily.

May all that you seek come to you in perfect time and deep alignment with your reason for incarnating this time. And may you enjoy all you receive with an open and grateful heart.

Y A'ho

— BLESSING —
Thanksgiving

To express gratitude and honor abundance

Thanksgiving is the time to lovingly express our gratitude for the abundance in our lives. Repeat this blessing aloud during your Thanksgiving ritual to inspire your own gratitude for all you have cultivated this year.

Great Spirit, Mother Earth,
Father God, Source of All That Is,
Today we give thanks for your abundant
*   blessings.*
We thank you for the gifts of the Earth,
which sustain us and grace us with beauty
*   each day.*
For this home and table,
where we are held and gather today.
For this food of the land,
which nourishes our bodies and warms
*   our souls.*

We thank you for the gift of community,
which connects us and holds us in this life.
For our family of birth and of choice,
who nurture and love us through the
*   passing years.*
For friends far and wide,
for their companionship and joy.
We thank you for the gift of this day,
and honor you with the gratitude in
*   our hearts.*
We are so grateful for this gathering,
for loved ones who make sure we never
*   walk alone.*
And most of all, for this life,
with its infinite gifts of joy, grace, and love.
For these, and all of our blessings,
we offer our gratitude on this day of
*   Thanksgiving.*
And we ask for continued blessings
upon us and all we love.

Amen, A'ho, So it is

— OFFERING —
Universal Prayer

To hold space for planetary healing and peace at the holidays

*Great Spirit, we come to you in many
    forms today.
From all traditions, races, countries,
ethnicities, and belief systems
with one intention:
to hold space for those who are in need.
Those whose bodies and spirits have
    been wounded,
and those whose hearts are aching—
the lonely, the weak, the disheartened.
We come as Spirit Warriors
to guide them, to hold them,
to love them, to raise them up,
and to offer them solace
in an energetic embrace
during this sacred season of hope.
An embrace that will encircle them*

*in every country, space, and nation.
Today, Great Spirit, I ask that you wrap
    those in need
in bundles of comfort and light,
fueled by the warmth of your spirit.
Help them feel and know
that kindred around the world
are holding them tightly.
May their pain know an end
and may they be healed swiftly.
We hold this intention with faith
    and gratitude
for your presence in the midst of
    our circle.
We are all One, and when one hurts,
we all hurt.
But when one is healed,
all are healed.*

Amen, Aho, So it is

— Project 20 —
11/11 (November 11)
Wishing Scroll Ritual

To attract all that you seek while doors to wealth are open

This is a wishing ritual, best performed on the 11th day of November, when energies of divine synchronicity are especially active.

Gather:
- 2 white candles to represent 11
- 2 crystals aligned to your desires (should be the same stone)
- White sage, copal, or palo santo for smudging
- Perfume or essential oil blend for attraction (e.g., bay, catnip, melissa, clary sage, and neroli)
- A piece of paper, 8½ × 11 inches (21.6 × 28 cm)
- A pen
- Ribbon

Place your candles to the east and west of your altar or sacred space. Position your crystals next to the candles, and smudge everything. Anoint yourself and your space if you feel called with your oil blend. Beginning at the top left corner of your paper, fill it with your desires, needs, and deepest inner longings. Don't be shy. Ask for what you seek for yourself, for your inner child, for your inner crone. Ask for what you need as a wife, husband, partner, father, mother, brother, sister, friend. Do you desire space or connection? Travel or more time at home?

Dream big, reaching into your memory to locate the places and moments where you felt *not heard* or not seen. Make wishes to heal those hidden places. What medicine is needed in the dark corners of your soul, what in the brightly illuminated garden of your mind?

At the bottom right corner of your paper, write, "It is done. Thank you thank you thank you." Roll your paper into a scroll, tying loosely with ribbon. May the process and the outcome bless you equally.

Amen, A'ho, So it is

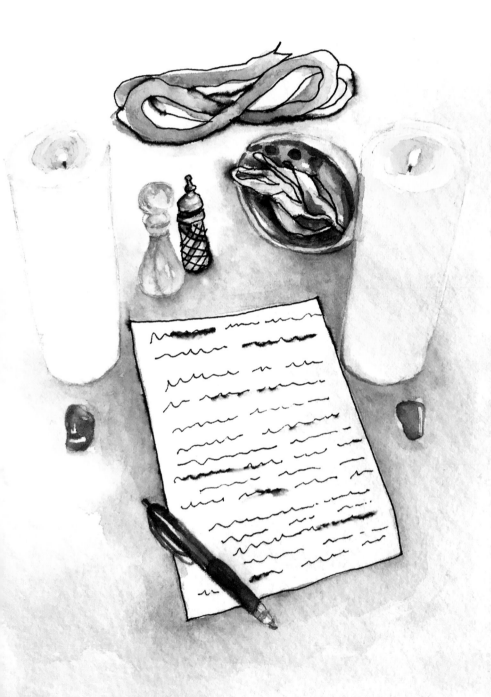

— Project 21 —
Gratitude Altar

To remind you to stay in a space of grateful joy

In November, there is an energy of gratitude in the air. It's the perfect time to build a gratitude altar.

Gather:

- A seasonal altar covering if you like
- Palo santo, copal, or white sage for smudging
- A brown or gold candle or tealights
- A seasonal blend of essential oils (e.g., clove, cardamom, cinnamon cassia, blood orange, and styrax)
- Crystals of abundance and gratitude (e.g., pyrite, citrine, selenite, amethyst, and lapis lazuli)
- Small pumpkins or gourds to represent abundance
- Fall leaves for decoration and adornment (optional)

A gratitude altar can be placed anywhere in your home. Add your covering and make sure the space is clean. Bring your attention to your breath, and focus your thoughts for 5 minutes on all of the things that you are grateful for: the people, experiences, and places that bring color and meaning to your world. Smudge your space and then place your candle in the southernmost corner to represent fire. Place your oil blend in the west to represent water and flow. Add your crystals and gourds to the northern edge of your altar to represent earth. And finally, place your smudging herbs and a few fallen leaves on the eastern side to represent air. From here you can embellish, add, and move items to make the space aesthetically pleasing.

Once your altar looks balanced and beautiful, it is complete! Leave it up for the month, the entire season, or even the entire year!

Amen, A'ho, So it is

— PROJECT 22 —
Karmic Release Offerings

To let go of disease, illness, and anger energies of the past

With this project you will create intentional offerings designed to detach karmic bonds that anchor you to experiences that are not in alignment with your Highest Good. Energetic bonds and attachments can be very strong, even across generations and even if you did not seek or affirm them.

What are the patterns you need to break within your family lines to experience true healing and liberation? For example, if your family experienced war in recent generations, you likely have fear and anxiety imprinted in your energetic field.

You will only ever know part of the story. You have lived other lifetimes, after all. You will also want to reflect on them. An important part of this work is not releasing energies that are still teaching you in some way. Ask your spirit guides to assist you in discerning which energies to focus on. When you do this sacred work, you not only heal yourself, but you also heal the generations behind you and those still to come.

Gather:

- Herbs aligned to the energies you are releasing (e.g., rosemary or eucalyptus for releasing health problems; if there is a specific health energy you are shedding, see if you can find a more specific herb that corresponds to it or the area of the body it affects)
- Gemstones aligned to your releasing work (e.g., bronzite for surrendering with grace, chrysoprase for a broken heart)
- Perfumes or essential oils that correspond to what you are releasing
- A small bowl or offering dish, 2 to 4 inches (5 to 10 cm) in size
- A black candle

continued

Call in your healing guides and welcome them along with the elemental guardians to your healing space. Thank them for their presence and support. Ask them to work through your hands, freeing you to surrender circumstances and energies that are no longer aligned to your development. Give them permission to do so without your conscious awareness, if that feels right. Begin placing your herbs, crystals, and oils into your offering bowl, one by one. After each addition, say a quiet prayer thanking the offerings for helping you identify and release old patterns. Each item you add is holding space for your recovery, rebirth, and renewal. Light your black candle and drip one drop of wax onto the offering blend for each energy stream you are releasing. It might be a single drop of wax, or you might burn through your whole candle. You will know when enough wax has been spilled.

Now, find a place, in your own garden preferably, to bury these offerings. Even the roots of a potted plant will work. Open the earth with your hand in a clockwise motion, place the offerings, and then cover the earth with your hand in a counterclockwise motion. All the while, sing, give thanks, and pray. Your healing is already under way. Let it go, with grace and gratitude.

Amen, A'ho, So it is

— Project 23 —
Mulling Herbs

To scent your home, and for holiday gifting

Part of the magic of the holidays is those smells that remind you of home, connection, celebration, and togetherness. One way to bring the scents of fall into your home while also creating a sacred offering is to craft batches of mulling or simmering herbs that you can blend with apple cider or red wine to make a sweet-smelling and heartwarming beverage while also scenting your entire home for the season.

Gather:
- 24 cinnamon sticks
- 24 cardamom pods
- 2 ounces (56 g) clove buds
- 1 gingerroot, peeled and sliced
- 24 star anise pods
- 4 ounces (112 g) dried orange peel
- Organza bags for gifting (optional)
- A quartz point to charge your herbs, one per gift (optional)
- Ribbons or gift tags to adorn bags (optional)
- Notepaper
- Pen

Gather your ingredients, and take a moment to consider the energies they bring to your home this season. Cinnamon brings abundance, prosperity, and hope. Cardamom brings passion, connection, and encouragement. Clove is powerful for attraction and brings your desires to fruition. Ginger cleanses and detoxifies the mind, body, and spirit. Star anise is a powerful offering to Great Spirit, and brings clarity and balance. Orange peel brings financial abundance and happiness. As you combine these herbs, roots, and fruits together, using your hands, imagine the alchemy of these energies and how they will bless you, your loved ones, and those who receive them as a gift this season. Once you have combined all of the ingredients together, separate them into 4-ounce (112 g) servings (which will infuse two large batches of wine or cider), place them into organza bags with a quartz point to magnify the energies, and adorn with ribbons or gift tags. Place a note inside each bag with instructions for use. You can copy the text below as an example.

continued

Instructions for use:
Add 2 to 3 ounces (56 to 84 g) of mulling herbs to a tea strainer or reusable spice bag. Pour 24 ounces (710 ml) of apple cider or red wine into a Dutch oven or large saucepan. Add the tea strainer or spice bag. Simmer over low heat for at least 30 minutes to infuse flavors and up to 2 hours. Then, remove from the heat, strain any remaining herbs from the liquid, and serve warm.

Cheers to your health, happiness, and wealth this holiday season!

Amen, A'ho, So it is

As you combine these herbs, roots, and fruits together, using your hands, imagine the alchemy of these energies and how they will bless you, your loved ones, and those who receive them as a gift this season.

12 DECEMBER

THE MONTH OF GRACE

And then in December, a hush descends across the land. The turning of the Great Wheel from fall to winter brings a hush of stillness and permission to slow it all down. While family gatherings and travel plans can make this month stressful, December offers respite from the rush of the rest of the year. To the extent possible, carve out time and space for yourself and your loved ones. Light candles around your home and turn off the electronics every evening, gathering around the fireplace or Christmas tree.

The energy of December is connected to Christ Consciousness, which is the spirit of grace and loving-kindness that permeates our human existence. We often find ourselves in a more loving, generous, and open mood. We want to be more compassionate, giving, and forgiving of others. Our best selves emerge and hope is rekindled.

For those who have lost loved ones, December can be a difficult month. The antidote to sadness is service, so if your heart is hurting during the holiday season, find ways to engage in philanthropic efforts. Give your time to someone else who is also hurting or suffering in some way. The spirit of this month may help you find grace through service to others. Let the whole family participate in decorating your home or sacred space with natural, organic materials and lots of sparkling candlelight. Making your home magical at the holidays can be easy, fun, and affordable. Put the emphasis on time together and honoring sacred traditions; the more you rest and restore your soul now, the more prepared you will feel come spring. Enjoy the tender warmth of winter's embrace.

Y A'ho

— Blessing —
and Invocation
Christmas

A gathering of energies for rest and inner reflection

God, Source, Great Spirit,
on this day of Christ's birth
our spirits rejoice.
The birth of Christ brings us great
    hope.
For Jesus came to share light, love,
    and healing.
His is a message of forgiveness
and unconditional love.
Help me become a channel of
    Christ's light.
Help me walk my soul path with peace
within my heart and mind.

Living in His way,
I will love what is unlovable,
and forgive what is unforgivable.
Today is a day to share Christ
    Consciousness
with our beloveds, the spirit of pure
    generosity.
For when we give generously, generously
    we receive.
And when we love generously, generously
    we are loved.
May all be blessed with the spirit of peace
and the gladness of a full heart
during this sacred time of Christmas.

Amen, Aho, So it is

— Blessing —
and Invocation
Yule

A calling to honor the longest night of the year

As we approach the end of our calendar year and the many holy days around the world, Yule is a grand turning point, a moment to pause and acknowledge the sacredness of these days.

*Great Spirit, Mother Earth, and
  Father Sky,
As we celebrate this day of Yule,
with its festive music, lights, and feasts,
we honor the passing of our sacred
  winter solstice,
and watch in awe as the Great Wheel
  turns toward winter.
Through the longest of nights,
please help our bodies find rest in
  the stillness,
our souls find wisdom in the silence,*

*and our hearts find hope in the sky's
  brightest star.
Through the coldest of days,
as we call back the warmth of the sun's
  bright light,
may we rejoice in the year's abundant
  blessings,
and be grateful for the lessons embodied
  in our losses.
For Yule is both a beginning and
  an end,
the darkness and the light, our year
  divided in two.
Our commitments for this year sealed,
  finished,
our plans for the year ahead unfolding,
  becoming.
Bless us as we heal within
during this season of rest.*

Amen, Aho, and So it is

— PROJECT 24 —
Sacred Yule Votive

To light your way through the dark months

During the dark days of winter, candlelight becomes a source of illumination and hope. Light brings with it possibility, beauty, and a sense of alignment.

Gather:
- A glass votive holder
- A rubber band
- Cinnamon sticks
- Sprigs of holly, mistletoe, pine, or other holiday greenery
- Herbs such as white sage, rosemary, mugwort, cypress, or juniper
- Velvet or textured ribbons
- Scissors
- Chip stones or small quartz points for decorating (optional)
- Tealight
- A lighter

This project is best done at the waxing or new moon, when you have the strongest energetic opportunity to set a new vision or new course for your life, or when you are building energy toward your dreams. Alternatively, craft your votive at the full moon to celebrate the fruition of dreams past and present.

Hold your glass votive and say a gratitude blessing for the light it will hold and the container it will offer. Place a rubber band around the center of the votive holder. Place the cinnamon sticks, sprigs, and herbs vertically against your votive holder, under the rubber band.

Tie your ribbon(s) around the center of your votive, over the sticks and branches. Let the long ends hang down and trim any excess. Then, cut the rubber band away. Optionally, affix chip stones or other decor to your votive. Add a tealight and light it. Ask that its light be a source of peace, hope, and happiness for all who see it. You are ready to add this magical votive to your sacred space or anywhere you will enjoy the light it casts.

Amen, A'ho, So it is

— Project 25 —
Yule Ritual

To retreat and receive the gifts of the spirit

The longest night of the year warrants a powerful ritual. All signs in nature point to the need for you to rest and conserve your resources. The only growth that happens now is inner growth, the growth of the soul; but that growth is also the most important. For this ritual, the focus is on receiving gifts of the spirit—your psychic and intuitive gifts. These gifts are known as *clairaudience*, or clear hearing; *clairsentience*, or clear sensing; *clairvoyance*, or clear sight; and *clairalience*, or clear smelling. Spirit communicates through these senses. The more finely tuned yours become, the more likely you will be to activate spirit wisdom in your life.

continued

Gather:

- Palo santo, copal, or white sage for smudging
- An indigo candle for activating your Third Eye chakra
- A white candle to represent inner stillness and peace
- A perfume or an oil blend aligned to psychic development (e.g., cypress, mugwort, rose, or opoponax)
- 4 crystals, one to represent each of the soul gifts you will develop during this ritual (Crystals of the Third Eye chakra are good options here: lapis lazuli, sapphire, iolite, and tanzanite, as are any stones from the zeolite family, such as scolecite and apophyllite, which activate all upper chakras.)
- A notebook

Smudge your space. Place your candles in the southern quadrant of your altar, and light both to usher in peace and open your Seeing Eye. Anoint yourself and your crystals if you feel called, using your psychic development blend or just a single essential oil note. Decide based on your intuition which crystal will represent each of the soul gifts: clairaudience, clairvoyance, clairsentience, and clairalience. Take each crystal, one by one, and call upon your spirit guides to reveal some new aspect of each gift today. In what ways can your senses of sight, understanding, hearing, and smell become more accurate sources of information, not only from this dimension but also from the universe as a whole?

As you go, make notes in your journal about your experiences. Even tiny shifts in perception are worth noting, as your soul gifts tend to develop incrementally. By becoming more conscious of your gifts, you will come into deeper awareness and appreciation of them.

Once you have meditated with each of the four crystals and recorded your experiences, take a deep breath and give thanks to your spirit allies for their support. Keep these stones with you, separate from your others, for they now have a specific charge and frequency. May they continue to show you ways to deepen your wisdom and expand your gifts, now at Yule and always.

Amen, A'ho, So it is

Conclusion and Closing Prayer

As you enjoy these ancient rituals and learn to craft magic with your own hands, you step into a long lineage of healers and medicine people who have worked hard to carry these traditions forward. We stand in their footsteps and we are grateful. A'ho.

When you finish a ceremony, ritual, or craft of any kind, give thanks for what you have learned or received, even if you feel like you have already expressed gratitude. Then, acknowledge the beauty of what has been with clarity and honesty. Sometimes beauty is indulgent and luxurious; other times, beauty is overwhelming and even scary. We may not know how to work with or sit with beauty. But the process of learning brings us closer to Source, to God, and to our own true nature. We are simply sentient extensions of divine consciousness. Part of that consciousness is the presence to all of creation—the birth *and* the death, the beginning *and* the ending. In magical work, we close circles counterclockwise—*widdershins*, or against the sun—to acknowledge the unwinding of energy that accompanies the completion of ritual. As we turn away from the sunshine of this book in these closing words, take a moment here to honor what you have learned and received from this book. Energetically, you have also brought your own magic and energy to this book, and for that may you also be blessed in all ways, always.

Amen, A'ho, and On we go

Acknowledgments

Many people worked hard to make this beautiful book a reality. First, thanks go to Jill Alexander, my editor, and Tiffany Hill who edited the book gracefully, allowing all the original content to find its way into the final version. Thanks as well to John Gettings for managing the project through to completion, and to Regina Grenier for her skilled leadership of the art design process. I also want to thank Team SG and Becca, in particular, for her stunning photography, which formed the foundation of the incredible illustration of the book by artist Andrea Henning; and the design by Tina Berning. Thank you to all of you for your vision, integrity, and beauty, and most of all for your support.

To the reader, you are entering a sacred chamber by reading this book, a vault of wisdom that for many remains secret. For thousands of years, magical invocations and blessings were shared in oral traditions but not archived the way they are here. Each time you sit with this book, take it as an opportunity to connect with your own ancestral and magical lineage. In that way you will personalize your experience of these words and their energy will have a more profound impact on you and your practice. May it be so.

To my husband, Dave, my children, Nick and Zoe, and my parents, Nick and Marie, thank you for supporting and encouraging me through this process. BrookeLynn, Sona, and Claire, thank you for your leadership and your inspiration. To my teachers along the way whose wisdom has been a source of inspiration and transformation, thank you for your magic. And to my students—past, present, and future—I wrote these words for you. I gathered these blessings, invocations, and rituals like flowers with which to craft a bouquet of beauty for your nourishment and pleasure. May you receive my words in that spirit. Amen, A'ho, So it is.

In your service, with gratitude,

Athena

About the Author

Athena Perrakis, Ph.D., is the best-selling author of *The Ultimate Guide to Chakras* and *Crystal Lore, Legends & Myths.* Founder and chief executive officer of Sage Goddess, the world's largest source of sacred tools and metaphysical education. Each week, Sage Goddess reaches more than two million people across the globe, on every continent and in more than sixty countries. She holds a Ph.D. from the University of Southern California in educational leadership, and has fifteen years of experience as a professor, corporate trainer and consultant, and educator. Athena has traveled the globe and worked with CEOs and senior executives from the Fortune 500 companies. But her metaphysical experience, in which her current work is largely rooted, spans more than three decades. During that time, she has become an expert in gemology, astrology, Tarot, aromatherapy, Reiki, and herbal medicine. Her Etsy shop was the first online metaphysical storefront to achieve top-10 store status in the handmade category around the world. Today, there are more than 5,000 products available through SageGoddess.com—everything from essential oils and ritual perfumes to candles, jewelry, gemstones in every form, home decor, clothing, body art and temporary tattoos, canvas art, and more.

Other books by Athena Perrakis, Ph.D.

**The Ultimate Guide
to Chakras**
978-1-59233-847-4

**Crystal Lore, Legends
& Myths**
978-1-59233-841-2

The Chakras Handbook
978-1-59233-875-7

Quarto
Knows

Inspiring | Educating | Creating | Entertaining

Brimming with creative inspiration, how-to projects, and useful
information to enrich your everyday life, Quarto Knows is a favorite
destination for those pursuing their interests and passions. Visit our
site and dig deeper with our books into your area of interest:
Quarto Creates, Quarto Cooks, Quarto Homes, Quarto Lives,
Quarto Drives, Quarto Explores, Quarto Gifts, or Quarto Kids.

© 2019 Quarto Publishing Group USA Inc.
Text © 2019 Athena Perrakis, Ph.D.

First Published in 2019 by Fair Winds Press, an imprint of The Quarto Group,
100 Cummings Center, Suite 265-D, Beverly, MA 01915, USA.
T (978) 282-9590 F (978) 283-2742 QuartoKnows.com

All rights reserved. No part of this book may be reproduced in any form without written permission of the
copyright owners. All images in this book have been reproduced with the knowledge and prior consent of the
artists concerned, and no responsibility is accepted by producer, publisher, or printer for any infringement
of copyright or otherwise, arising from the contents of this publication. Every effort has been made to ensure
that credits accurately comply with information supplied. We apologize for any inaccuracies that may have
occurred and will resolve inaccurate or missing information in a subsequent reprinting of the book.

Fair Winds Press titles are also available at discount for retail, wholesale, promotional, and bulk purchase.
For details, contact the Special Sales Manager by email at specialsales@quarto.com or by mail at The
Quarto Group, Attn: Special Sales Manager, 100 Cummings Center, Suite 265-D, Beverly, MA 01915, USA.

23 22 21 20 19   1 2 3 4 5

ISBN: 978-1-59233-877-1

Digital edition published in 2019

Library of Congress Cataloging-in-Publication Data available

Design: Tina Berning
Cover Image: sagegoddess
Page Layout: Tina Berning
Illustration: Andrea Henning
Background Textures: © Shutterstock.com

Printed in China

MIX
Paper from
responsible sources
FSC
www.fsc.org   FSC® C008047